Contents

Volume 16, Number 1 -- Fall 2008

From the Editor 5
By Andreea Serban

The Effect of Tutoring on Student Success 6
By James Kostecki & Trudy Bers

This research examined the effect of tutoring on student success at an open enrollment community college, controlling for gender, age, race/ethnicity, highest level of education, and reading, writing and mathematics competency. Student success was defined three ways: term grade point average (GPA), success in courses, and persistence from the fall to spring semesters. Using analysis of variance and logistic regression, researchers found that tutoring was associated with student success, controlling for the other variables. Results provide empirical support for the hypothesized importance of tutoring in colleges' arsenals of student support services.

Effects of Learning-Style Responsive Versus Traditional Staff Development on Community College Professors' Attitudes Toward Alternative Instructional Strategies 13
By Christina T. Hart & Rita Dunn

How does one know whether traditional or innovative staff development is working? This study compared the effects of professors' attitudes toward learning through traditional staff development versus alternative instructional strategies for teaching community college students. Eight-four professors participated in this study. The average participant was a White female between the ages of 40-49 who taught in the departments of Arts and Sciences. For this study the participants attended workshops focused on three different instructional strategies for teaching college students – Programmed Learning Sequences (PLS), Team Learning (TL), and Circle of Knowledge (COK). These three strategies were taught in a counter-balanced design. Thus, each group of faculty was taught with both a traditional and a learning-style approach, but in a different sequence so that each group served as its own control in a repeated measures design. The Productivity Environmental Preference Survey (PEPS) identified the participants' learning styles. The Semantic Differential Scale (SDS) (Pizzo, 1981) assessed their attitudes toward each of the two different instructional approaches. The community college faculty's attitudes significantly ($p <.05$) favored the learning-styles responsive approach over the traditionally taught workshop regardless of the content.

Application of Survival Analysis to Study Timing and Probability of Outcome Attainment by a Community College Student Cohort 22
By Roger Mourad & Ji-Hee Hong

This study applies competing risks survival analysis to describe outcome attainment for an entire cohort of students who first attended a Midwestern community college in the Fall Semester 2001. Outcome attainment included transfer to a four-year institution, degree/certificate attainment from the community college under study, and transfer to a different two-year college. The analysis also shows how the technique can be used to categorize students who have not realized a graduation or transfer outcome. Outcome probability at different points in time (13 semesters) is calculated and discussed. The effects of demographic and academic variables on timing and type of outcome attained are also discussed. Findings from the study show that outcome attainment was widely distributed over chronological time, there were three discernable stages of outcome attainment across number of semesters enrolled, and cumulative grade point average (GPA) was the most prominent effect on outcome.

Who Are Our Students? Cluster Analysis as a Tool for Understanding Community College Student Populations 32
By Bridget V. Ammon, Jamillah Bowman & Roger Mourad

This study showcases cluster analysis as a useful tool for those who seek to understand the types of students their community colleges serve. Although educational goal, academic program, and demographics are often used as descriptive variables, it is unclear which, if any, of these are the best way to classify community college students. Cluster analyses at two points in time each identified nine distinct clusters in our data. These clusters had a 67% overlap, indicating method validity and consistency over time. The differences between the two years could be due to differences in enrollment over time, but are likely a result of changes in questions asked of the students from year one to year two. The results of this study suggest the utility of cluster analysis as a way for stakeholders to describe and classify their students. Furthermore, once established, cluster membership can be used to predict later success, usage of student services, and other important outcomes. When administrators understand these differences among students, they can better serve all groups of students and identify ways to market to them and address their unique needs.

Peer Grouping: The Refinement of Performance Indicators 45
By Willard Hom

Community colleges operate under much scrutiny these days, and these institutions have experienced a growing emphasis on performance indicators as paths to institutional accountability. California's system of 109 community colleges recently developed and implemented an innovative accountability program that used peer group comparison as one of its elements. This article describes California's use of peer grouping in terms of its development, mechanics, and implications for the future.

A Methodology for Generating Placement Rules that Utilizes Logistic Regression 52
By Keith Wurtz

The purpose of this article is to provide the necessary tools for institutional researchers to conduct a logistic regression analysis and interpret the results. Aspects of the logistic regression procedure that are necessary to evaluate models are presented and discussed with an emphasis on cutoff values and choosing the appropriate number of candidate predictor variables. In order to demonstrate the process of conducting a logistic regression analysis, models are generated using educational background measures (e.g., last grade in English, high school grade point average, etc.) to predict the dichotomous outcome of success (i.e., grade of A, B, C, or CR) in an English course. At the same time, the information presented here can be applied to other logistic regression studies. Topics covered include setting up the database, dummy coding, data reduction, multicollinearity, missing cases, setting the cutoff value, interpretation of the results, selecting a model, and the interpretation of odds ratios when they are negative.

Current Lit Abstracts: The Influence of Financial Aid on Community College Students 59
By Eddy A. Ruiz

The following citations for research and resource materials focus on the influence of financial aid on community college students.

Book Review 63
By Bill Scroggins

2008 Annual Update of the Journal of Applied Research 65
By Andreea M. Serban

President's Message 67
By Georgia Gudykunst

The Journal of Applied Research in the Community College

is a semi-annual journal published jointly by

The National Community College Council for Research and Planning
and New Forums Press, Inc.

PUBLISHER: Douglas Dollar
CIRCULATION: Jean McKinley

EXECUTIVE EDITOR:
Andreea M. Serban, President/Superintendent, Santa Barbara City College (CA)

ASSOCIATE EDITORS:
Susan Bach, Portland, OR
Maureen Pettitt, Director of Institutional Research, Skagit Valley College (WA)
Marc Beam, Director of Institutional Research, Kern Community College District (CA)
Barbara McNeice-Stallard, Director of Research and Institutional Effectiveness, Mt. San Antonio College (CA)

MANAGING EDITOR:
Diane Riopka, Technology & Learning Services, South Orange County Community College District (CA)

SPONSORING ORGANIZATIONS:
Consortium for Community College Development

SUBSCRIPTIONS: The Journal is published semiannually in September and February each year. Subscription rates are $35.00 per year. AACC-affiliated councils may purchase group subscriptions for their membership at a special rate of $17.50 by making prior arrangements with the publisher. For further information on subscribing, to include arrangements for site licenses, contact New Forums Press, P.O. Box 876 Stillwater, OK 74076: Phone 405-372-6158: FAX 405-377-2237.

SUBMISSIONS: The National Community College Council for Research and Planning and New Forums Press invite manuscripts for JARCC. The Purpose of this biannual journal is to serve the needs and interests of institutional researchers and planners in the community colleges well as those of administrators, faculty, policy makers and others with an interest in the community college. For more information and submission guidelines, see *information for contributors* at the back of this journal.

COPYRIGHT © 2008 by New Forums Press. Inc. All Rights Reserved.

Editorial Advisory Board

Trudy Bers
Executive. Director, Institutional Research, Curriculum and Planning
Oakton Community College (IL)

Kathleen Bigsby
Director, Institutional Analysis and Planning
Kwantlen University College (BC)

Karl Boughan
Senior Analyst, Office of Planning & Institutional Research
Prince George's Community College (MD)

Debra Bragg
Professor and Director of Community College Research and Leadership
University of Illinois at Urbana-Champaign (IL)

Harriott Calhoun
Director, Institutional Research and Information Services
Jefferson State Community College (AL)

Patricia Carter
Executive Director, Consortium for Community College Development
Center for the Study of Postsecondary and Higher Education
School of Education,
University of Michigan (MI)

Christine Cress
Associate Professor, Postsecondary, Adult and Continuing Education
Graduate School of Education,
Portland State University (OR)

James Goho
Director, Research and Planning
Red River College (MB)

Linda Hagedorn
Chair, Education Administration and Policy Department
College of Education,
University of Florida (FL)

Thomas C. Henry
President
Mohave Community College (AZ)

Dorsey Kendrick
President
Gateway Community College (CT)

Mark Oromaner
1 Washington Square Village
New York, NY 10021 (NY)

Daniel Phelan
President
Jackson Community College (MI)

Laura Saunders
Vice President of Administration
Bellevue Community College (WA)

Jeffrey Seybert
Director of Research, Planning and Resource Development
Johnson County Community College District (KS)

Julie Slark
Assistant Vice Chancellor of Educational Services
Rancho Santiago Community College District (CA)

Greg P. Smith
Executive Vice President
Central Community College (NE)

Jacki Stirn
Retired/Consultant
Greenwood Village (CO)

Patricia Windham
Associate Vice-Chancellor for Evaluation
Florida Department of Education, Division of Community Colleges and Workforce Education
Florida State Board of Community Colleges (FL)

Abstracts and Indexes: *The Journal of Applied Research in the Community College* is abstracted or indexed in Current Index to Journals in Education and Higher Education Abstracts.

Executive Editor's Note: Advisory Board members do not necessarily endorse the opinion or research methods presented in articles published by the Journal. The Executive Editor takes sole responsibility for manuscript selection and editorial quality.

From the Editors...

We are pleased to present a new JARCC issue. Included in this issue are articles by *James Kostecki and Trudy Bers*, "The Effect of Tutoring on Student Success"; *Christina T. Hart and Rita Dunn*, "Effects of Learning-Style Responsive Versus Traditional Staff Development on Community College Professors' Attitudes Toward Alternative Instructional Strategies"; *Roger Mourad and Ji-Hee Hong*, "Application of Survival Analysis to Study Timing and Probability of Outcome Attainment by a Community College Student Cohort"; and *Bridget V. Ammon, Jamillah Bowman, and Roger Mourad*, "Who Are Our Students? Cluster Analysis as a Tool for Understanding Community College Student Populations". The editorial team is pleased with the high quality and breadth of articles included in this issue. We hope you will enjoy reading them.

There are two Toolbox articles in this issue by *Willard Hom*, "Peer Grouping: The Refinement of Performance Indicators"; and *Keith Wurtz*, "A Methodology for Generating Placement Rules that Utilizes Logistic Regression." *Eddy Ruiz* provided a compilation of abstracts of several publications and reports dealing with the impact of financial aid on community college students. *Bill Scroggins* reviewed "Achieving and Sustaining Institutional Excellence for the First Year of College" written by Betsy O. Barefoot, John N. Gardner, Marc Cutright, Libby V. Morris, Charles C. Schroeder, Stephen W. Schwartz, Michael J. Siegel, and Randy L. Swing.

Annual reports from the *JARCC* editors and NCCCRP Past President Georgia Gudykunst conclude this issue. As always, the editors appreciate the hard work of each of the authors as they responded to our questions and finalized their manuscripts for publication.

We would like to acknowledge the contribution made by Marc Beam, who served as Associate Editor. Denice Inciong, Director of Research and Planning at South Orange County Community College District in Mission Viejo, California will replace Marc starting with the work for the Spring 2009 issue.

Please feel free to contact any of the editors about your interest in publication and what might be involved in turning your local research into a publishable article. Information about submitting articles is included at the end of this issue. We also encourage letters to the editor or other types of articles that may help to inform and improve the practice of institutional research, planning and assessment in community colleges. We look forward to hearing from you!

Andreea Serban, Ph.D.
Executive Editor
JARCC

The Effect of Tutoring on Student Success

James Kostecki
American Academy of Dermatology

Trudy Bers
Oakton Community College

This research examined the effect of tutoring on student success at an open enrollment community college, controlling for gender, age, race/ethnicity, highest level of education, and reading, writing and mathematics competency. Student success was defined three ways: term grade point average (GPA), success in courses, and persistence from the fall to spring semesters. Using analysis of variance and logistic regression, researchers found that tutoring was associated with student success, controlling for the other variables. Results provide empirical support for the hypothesized importance of tutoring in colleges' arsenals of student support services.

Introduction and Purpose

During the past 10 years, there has been increased national attention directed to student success in higher education. Emanating from a variety of sources, including calls for accountability, revised accreditation criteria that place greater emphasis on student outcomes, and greater emphasis on teaching *and learning*, colleges are expected to do a more substantial job of measuring students' learning and using assessment results for improvement. The recent report of the Spellings Commission and spring 2007 Department of Education negotiated regulations discussions regarding the possible role of accrediting agencies in guaranteeing institutional performance further underscore the expectation that colleges will need to be able to document student success. How colleges can affect and improve learning and student success continues to be an unanswered question, although a variety of relatively new instruments and initiatives are aimed at this goal.

For example, the Foundations of Excellence® Project, sponsored by the Policy Center on the First Year of College, posits nine foundational dimensions of excellence, aspirational dimensions that characterize excellent college principles and programs for first-year and new college students. Two versions of the dimensions exist, one for four-year and the other for two-year colleges (Foundations of Excellence®, 2005).

The National Survey of Student Engagement (NSSE) and Community College Survey of Student Engagement (CCSSE) are both designed to obtain self-reported measures of student engagement; i.e., students respond to questions that assess institutional practices and student behaviors that research has shown to be correlated highly with student learning and student retention. National results provide an interesting picture of how students spend their time, particularly in activities identified as "good practices" in undergraduate education (CCSSE, 2007).

Achieving the Dream is another broad student success initiative. Now in its fourth year, the project involves more than 80 colleges in 15 states in multi-year efforts to improve student achievement, especially for low-income and minority students. Nearly all Achieving the Dream institutions are community colleges. Participating institutions are required to compile and analyze data on student performance to aid in developing intervention strategies that address what each institution identifies as critical barriers to success for its students. The colleges are expected to measure the impact of their strategies by compiling and analyzing data to determine whether students are, indeed, achieving at higher levels than had been the case before the new strategies were implemented (Achieving the Dream, 2006).

What these and other efforts share is a number of assumptions about the institutional policies and programs that foster student success. These policies and programs include placement in appropriate level mathematics and composition courses, required advising, orientation programs, provision of support services such as tutoring and mentoring, and both in-class and out-of-class activities that engage students rather than permitting them to be passive learners. What is relatively new, however, is research that tests the efficacy of these strategies.

The purpose of this project is to examine the efficacy of one common student success strategy: tutoring. Specifically, this study examined the achievement of students who received tutoring compared to similar students who did not, in order to examine the relationship between tutoring and performance.

Literature Review

A number of important studies have investigated factors that influence student success. In his seminal 1987 book, *Leaving College: Rethinking the Causes and Cures for*

Student Attrition, Tinto suggested that students who integrated both academically and socially into an institution were more likely to persist. Numerous subsequent studies have tested the validity of Tinto's theory with mixed results (Braxton, 2004). In their review of decades of research on the impact of college on students, Pascarella and Terenzini (2005) note several categories of theories about college student change: developmental, sociological, and environmental. Their work emphasizes that changes which occur in college come about from multiple experiences and can be viewed through different lenses. Thus colleges designing programs to foster student success need to take a broad perspective, recognizing that no single program or intervention will be effective for all students. Kuh and his colleagues (2007) prepared an extensive study summarizing research related to student success. They identified five theoretical perspectives: sociological, organizational, psychological, cultural and economic. In their work they also explored institutional initiatives affecting success, including academic support services. The literature they examined found many students did not use support services, but those who did were more likely to persist and earn higher grades (p. 87).

A small number of recent studies have empirically examined factors associated with student success in community colleges. For example, Jenkins et. al. (2006) looked at transcript-level data for 150,000 students in three cohorts of Florida community college students and conducted case studies of six colleges, three identified as "high impact" and three as "low impact." They identified seven sets of activities hypothesized to characterize effective colleges; i.e., institutions that had a high impact on student success. Jenkins and his colleagues concluded that high impact colleges targeted support for minority students, made them feel welcome, and offered programs and services targeted to them. Case studies of three high-impact and three low-impact colleges revealed general but not complete consistency between college practices and activities hypothetically associated with success.

Purnell and Blank (2004) suggested a number of support services that could help community college students succeed. These are clustered in five broad areas: academic guidance and counseling, personal guidance and counseling, career counseling, academic tutoring, and supplemental supports such as transportation and child care. They described a variety of such programs and presented an overview of several empirical studies of multi-service program effectiveness. However, they acknowledged that the research was based on descriptive and correlational studies rather than on rigorous research designs with control groups.

The Opening Doors Demonstration is a new, multi-college project to test the effectiveness of various intervention programs intended to improve student achievement and persistence (Brock & LeBlanc, 2005). The project involves random assignment of students to programmatic interventions, thus permitting researchers to gauge the impact of interventions while controlling for a variety of variables. To date, available empirical research examined the effect of learning communities at Kingsborough Community Colleges (Bloom & Sommo, 2005). Researchers found that students enrolled in learning communities outperformed control group students during their first semester and, one year after enrollment, were more likely to have completed remedial English requirements. Because Opening Doors uses random assignments of students, research from this project is likely to be of unusual value in assessing the effectiveness of intervention strategies.

At Washtenaw Community College in Michigan, researchers found that the odds of success in courses for students not tutored was 1.3 times as high as for students who were tutored, although variables were not used to control for differences between the two groups (Washtenaw Community College, 2006). No difference in success rates were found based on number of tutoring sessions.

Patton, Morelon, Whitehead, and Hossler (2006) examined published research on retention efforts to find examples of empirical evidence to support assumptions about program effectiveness. They concluded that "one of the most important findings of this investigation is the dearth of evidence to support the claims proffered on the efficacy of a wide range of campus-based retention initiatives" (p. 10). The authors also noted that few empirical studies had been conducted at community colleges.

Luan (2006) conducted a longitudinal study to assess the effect of tutoring on student success in courses. Using student information system data, Luan tracked students from Spring 1999 to Spring 2005. He found that students who enrolled in LIBR 502, an elective course that offers drop-in tutorial assistance, had higher rates of success in their courses than students who did not obtain this assistance. In particular, pre-collegiate basic skills students and younger students benefited most from tutoring.

Finally, McClenney, Marti, and Adkins (2007) linked the results from the CCSSE and institution-level data to confirm that students' self-reports of engagement and institutional practices were positively associated with a number of academic success measures, including GPA, percent of credits completed, and persistence from fall-to-spring and fall-to-fall terms.

While the literature about student success is large and growing, much of it is premised on studies conducted at four-year colleges and universities. Studies of support services and institutional practices intended to improve success tend to be more descriptive than analytical, so that the actual effectiveness of these measures continues to be largely unknown.

Methodology

This study was conducted at an open enrollment community college in the suburbs of a major metropolitan area. The population included the 2,724 students who were new to the college in Fall 2005. The central variable of interest was participation in tutoring (number of visits and total time in minutes for the semester). A number of student demographic and academic preparedness variables were used as controls (gender, age, race/ethnicity, placement into remedial math and English, highest level of study achieved to date). Three outcome measures of student success were used: fall term GPA, percent of fall courses successfully completed (grades of A, B, C, or Pass for remedial courses), and persistence to the spring semester. Because the college does not include remedial course grades in the calculation of GPAs, this variable by itself is an incomplete depiction of student success. Table 1 lists variables and descriptive statistics (frequency counts, means, and standard deviations).

To examine the association between success and tutoring, controlling for demographics and academic preparedness, we conducted a series of analyses using logistic regression to examine the effect of tutoring on the dependent variables persistence and course completion, and analysis of variance (ANOVA) to examine GPA. While some of the nominal variables, such as course placements, might masquerade as ordinal measures if we consider that remedial placements are lower than college-level placements, we could neither exclude the large number of students who had no placement data or make assumptions about what their placements might be. Therefore, we generated a series of dummy variables for writing, reading, and math placements and ethnicity. For writing and reading, variables were remedial placement (yes/no), college-level placement (yes/no), or no placement data. For math, variables were remedial placement (yes/no), intermediate algebra placement (yes/no), college-level placement (yes/no), or no placement data. For race/ethnicity, variables were white non-Hispanic (yes/no), minority (yes/no), or no information.

Successful course completion was initially defined as the percentage of courses successfully completed by each student. However, a large percentage of students took only one course and successfully completed it, skewing results in the direction of 100 percent. Therefore, each course was treated

Table 1. Control Variables, Tutoring and Outcome Variables

Categories	Number	Percent	Mean	SD
Gender				
Female	1,344	49.3		
Male	1,380	50.7		
Age				
Below 24	1,822	66.9		
24 or above	902	33.1		
Race/Ethnicity				
White Non-Hispanic	1,368	50.2		
Minority[a]	813	29.8		
Other/no information	543	19.9		
Highest Level Education				
Some college or below	2,143	78.7		
Associate's degree or higher	581	21.3		
Writing Placement				
Remedial	631	23.2		
College-level	801	29.4		
No placement test	1,292	47.4		
Reading Placement				
Remedial	600	22.0		
College-level reading course recommended	317	11.6		
No reading course needed	697	25.6		
No placement test	1,110	40.7		
Math Placement				
Remedial	853	31.3		
Intermediate algebra	301	11.0		
College-level math	222	8.1		
No placement test	1,348	49.5		
Received Tutoring				
Yes	306	11.2		
No	2,418	88.8		
Number Tutoring Visits (based on N=306)			4.7	6.6
Total Minutes Tutored (based on N=306)			297.6	518.3
Fall Grade Point Average[b]	2,282		2.38	1.33
Percent Courses Successfully Completed[c]	2,724		.65	.40
Returned Spring 2006 Semester				
Yes	1,688	.62		
No	1,036	.38		

[a] Includes Asian, Black, Hispanic, American Indian.
[b] 2,282 students earned grades of A, B, C, D, or F in at least one college-level course; remedial course grades are not included in GPA.
[c] Includes remedial and college-level courses with grades of A, B, C, or P divided by total number courses attempted in fall semester.

as a separate observation for each student and coded "1" if the grade was A, B, C, or P (pass in developmental courses) or "2" if the grade was D, F, incomplete, or withdrawal.

The frequency distribution for number of visits for tutoring also was highly skewed, with 2,418 students never obtaining tutoring, 125 students obtaining tutoring only once, 94 students obtaining tutoring two-four times, and the remaining 87 students obtaining tutoring five or more times. Consequently, we reclassified the number of tutoring visits into a dichotomous variable, where "0" equaled no visits and "1" equaled one or more visits.

Results

To investigate factors affecting the measures of student success, a univariate analysis for each success variable, each control variable, and the variable of interest (tutoring) was conducted to ascertain whether variables were differentially associated with success. T-tests or ANOVAs were used. As Table 2 indicates, tutoring and almost all control variables were statistically significant in their association with the student success indicators. The preliminary analysis also suggested that female students had higher term GPAs and higher rates of course success than male students. Older students had higher term GPAs and higher course success rates and were less likely to return in spring than younger students. Minority students had lower GPAs and were less likely to succeed than white students or those with unknown ethnicity. Students who placed in higher level math had higher term GPAs and were more likely to succeed in their courses and return in the spring term. Students who placed in higher level reading and writing had higher term GPAs and were more likely to return in the spring. Students who received tutoring were more successful in terms of successful course completions, term GPA, and persistence to the spring term than those who did not receive tutoring.

Statistical Models

The next step in the study was the creation of three statistical models—one for each success outcome—to examine the effect of tutoring net of other variables. A control variable was eliminated if it did not enter the model as statistically significant at the .05 alpha level. Control variables that were correlated with others were also eliminated from the model. Examining the relationships among the control variables, we found several such correlations: the highest level of education was correlated with age and placement levels (those with more education are more likely to be older and to either have no placement tests or to place into college-level courses), gender was correlated with age (women are more likely to be older), and placement in composition was correlated with placement in reading (students tend to place into college-level work in both areas, remedial work in both subjects, or to have no placement tests in both areas). The variable that had the greater contribution to the final model was retained.

Tutoring, the central variable of interest, was entered last to determine its effect, if any, on student success after controlling for other variables. After determining the final statistical model for each success outcome, the relative effect of each statistically significant variable on the outcome variable was examined. For those statistically significant control variables with multiple categories, we performed pairwise statistical tests to determine which levels predicted greater student success than other levels of that variable. For example, if math placement was statistically significant in predicting persistence to the spring term, which placement level(s)—remedial, intermediate algebra, college-level—predicted a higher likelihood of students enrolling in the spring?

Table 2. Relationship between Control Variables, Tutoring and Student Success

	Term GPA T-Test (T) or Analysis of Variance (F) Statistic	Successful Course Completion T-Test (T) or Analysis of Variance (F) Statistic	Persistence to Spring Chi-Square
Gender	6.15 (T)**	5.27 (T)**	1.19
Age	13.97 (T)**	5.50 (T)**	186.74**
Race/Ethnicity	12.86 (F)**	5.26 (F)*	11.90*
Highest Level of Education	14.46 (T)**	6.50 (T)**	154.56**
Placement in Reading	75.69 (F)**	2.08 (F)	477.59**
Placement in Writing	62.59 (F)**	0.25 (F)	361.62**
Placement in Math	59.16 (F)**	18.18 (F)**	366.79**
Received Tutoring	3.59 (T)**	5.35 (T)**	62.75**

*$p<.01$. **$p<.001$.

Model for Term Grade Point Average

Analysis of variance (ANOVA) was used to examine term GPA. All variables were found to be statistically significant. However, due to multicollinearity, placement in writing, age, and highest level of education were removed from the final model. Tutoring was entered into the model last and was found to be statistically significant. A pairwise comparison of every combination of levels within a variable was conducted to examine statistical differences in GPA. Table 3 displays the results of the final model.

The expected change in term GPA is interpreted as the expected difference in term GPA for students based on the variable of interest, after controlling for all other variables in the model. Overall, students who placed in remedial math have term GPAs that are .82 points lower than students who placed in college-level math, even adjusting for the effect of all other variables, including tutoring. The results indicate that tutoring does matter, however. Students who obtained tutoring have term GPAs .38 points higher than students who do not receive tutoring after controlling for the effects of race/ethnicity, gender, and course placements.

Model for Successful Course Completions

To examine successful course completions, a logistic regression analysis was employed using an event/trials form. For this model, an event was defined as the number of successful course completions and the trial was defined as the number of courses attempted in the term. Each control variable was found to be statistically significant; however, due to multicollinearity, placement in writing, age, and highest level of education were removed from the final model. Tutoring entered the model last and was also found to be statistically significant. A pairwise comparison of every combination of levels within a variable was conducted to examine statistical differences in successful course completion. Table 4 displays the results of the final course completion model.

The odds ratio is interpreted as the likelihood of a student successfully completing a course based on the variable of interest, after controlling for all other variables in the model. For example, students who placed in college level math were 2.8 times more likely than students who placed in remedial math to succeed in their courses, even adjusting for the effect of all other variables including tutoring. Note that all courses were examined, not just math courses. The results indicate that tutoring does matter: a student who obtained tutoring was 1.8 times as likely to successfully complete a course after controlling for the effects of race/ethnicity, gender, or course placements.

Model for Fall-to-Spring Persistence

To examine persistence to the spring semester, a logistic regression was used, with tutoring entered last. Gender was eliminated as not significant. A pairwise comparison of every combination of levels within a variable was conducted to examine statistical differences in persistence. Table 5 displays the results of the final persistence model.

The odds ratio is interpreted as the likelihood of a student persisting to spring based on the variable of interest, after controlling for all other variables in the model. For example, students who placed in college level reading were 4.5 times more likely than students with no placement test to persist to the spring semester, even adjusting for the effect of all other variables, including tutoring. In fact, students who did not take placement tests were less likely to persist even controlling for race/ethnicity and tutoring. Again, the results indicate that tutoring does matter. A student who obtained tutoring was 2.3

Table 3. Effects on Term GPA

Variable	Expected Change in Term GPA	95% Confidence Interval Lower	95% Confidence Interval Upper
Gender			
Female	0.31	0.20	0.41
Male			
Race / Ethnicity			
White	0.23	0.11	0.35
Minority			
Unknown	0.24	0.09	0.39
Placement in Reading			
2=College level			
1=Remedial	-0.37	-0.50	-0.23
0=No placement test	0.21	0.06	0.36
Placement in Math			
3=College level			
2=Intermediate algebra	-0.61	-0.83	-0.39
1=Remedial	-0.82	-1.02	-0.63
0=No placement test	-0.40	-0.61	-0.20
Received Tutoring			
Yes			
No	-0.38	-0.55	-0.22

times as likely to persist to the spring semester after controlling for the effects of race/ethnicity or course placements.

Limitations

This study has several limitations that should be acknowledged. This study was conducted at a single open-enrollment, commuter institution and the study's results may not be generalizable to dissimilar institutions. Also, several important potential contributors to student success—such as motivation, hours of employment, and family obligations—are not included in the models because data were not available. Grades, one of the dependent variables, may not be the best measure of student success, particularly if the focus is on learning itself. While grades or GPAs are not as pristine or pure a measure of what students know and can do as we might wish, they are widely used as success indicators. Finally, we were unable to operationally connect tutoring in a specific course or subject with academic success in that course. Instead, academic success is defined more globally for each student.

Discussion and Implications for Further Research

The results of this study suggest that tutoring is associated with student success as defined by GPA, successful completion of courses, and persistence to the next semester. This finding provides empirical evidence to support notions about the importance of including tutoring among the arsenal of student support services offered by community colleges. It may also strengthen the case for continuing financial support for tutoring, a service that rarely generates revenue.

However, the world of community colleges and community college students is far more complex than this simple study might suggest. Manny community college students must balance competing roles of student, employee, and family member. Fulfilling their multiple responsibilities may prevent them from taking full advantage of support services offered by a college, even when they recognize their academic performance might benefit from those services. Students may overestimate their knowledge and skills, assuming they will be able to succeed without assistance. Time management, the ability to complete assignments and prepare for examinations in a timely manner, is also a challenge for many students.

Table 4 Effects on Successful Course Completions

Variable	Odds Ratio	Most likely to succeed in course if...	Least likely to succeed in course if...
Gender		Female	Male
Female	1.4		
Male	--		
Race/ Ethnicity		Unknown	Minority
White	1.2		
Minority	--		
Unknown	1.4		
Placement in Math		College Level	Remedial
3=College level	2.8		
2=Intermediate algebra	1.4		
1=Remedial	--		
0= No placement test	1.3		
Received Tutoring	1.8	Yes	No

Table 5. Effects on Fall to Spring Persistence

Variable	Odds Ratio	Most likely to return in spring term if...	Least likely to return in spring term if...
Race/ Ethnicity		White or Minority	Unknown
White	1.4		
Minority	1.2		
Unknown	--		
Placement in Reading		College level	No placement test
2=College level	4.5		
1=Remedial	3.3		
0= No placement test	--		
Placement in Math		College level or Intermediate algebra	No placement test
3=College level	3.2		
2=Intermediate algebra	2.6		
1=Remedial	1.8		
0= No placement test	--		
Received Tutoring	2.3	Yes	No

Thus, despite evidence affirming the contribution of tutoring to student success, students may lack the time, recognition of need, or self-discipline to obtain tutoring.

Tutoring may also serve a different function for students: connecting them with the institution. While assisting them with the acquisition of knowledge and skills for success, tutoring may also link a student with someone who cares. This feeling of connection can be a crucial factor affecting students' experiences at a college, making them feel at home and encouraging persistence.

It may also be the case that the effect of tutoring is more granular than suggested by a success variable such as course success or GPA. Moving a student from a B to an A in the course will not change course success data, when success is defined as a grade of A, B, C, or Pass, for example. But to the student whose objective is to earn an A, tutoring can be as critical as for a student who wants only to earn a passing grade.

This study examines student success at the end of the term. It would be useful, perhaps, to examine changes in students' grades as they progress through the semester. This would require tracking both course performance and participation in tutoring during the semester and aligning performance on specific assignments with receipt of tutoring both in that specific course and for any course. Such a study would require faculty members to report grades on each course assignment by date, tutoring providers to report dates and subjects of tutoring, and researchers to link assignment grades and tutoring by date.

The effect of tutoring could also be explored through a longitudinal study to identify students who did not receive any tutoring in one term, but did receive tutoring in another, and to determine whether academic success differed based on whether or not they received any tutoring. This would be a pre-test, post-test design if the first term was the one in which tutoring was not received. Again, this may be an area for further research.

In a perfect research world, colleges could learn more about the direct effectiveness of tutoring by randomly assigning students to receive tutoring or not or by measuring other student characteristics such as motivation and external obligations. However, both ethics and the educational setting limit the feasibility of these approaches.

The value of the study reported in this article is that empirical evidence points to a clear relationship between tutoring and student success. That clear relationship may be causal for some or all students, but that is a statement we cannot make. Tutoring matters but, as of yet, research does not enable us to say exactly how.

References

Achieving the Dream. Retrieved June 14, 2007, from http://www.achievingthedream.org/ABOUTATD/OVERVIEW/default.tp

Bloom, D., and Sommo, C. (2005). *Building learning communities: Early results from the Opening Doors demonstration at Kingsborough Community College.* New York: MDRC.

Braxton, J, M., Hirschy, A, S, and McClendon, S, A. (2004). Toward understanding and reducing college student departure. *ASHE-ERIC Higher Education Report*, 30(3). San Francisco, CA: Jossey-Bass.

Brock, T., and LeBlanc, A. (2005). *Promoting student success in community college and beyond: The Opening Doors demonstration.* New York: MDRC.

Community College Survey of Student Engagement. (2006). *Act on Fact: Using Data to Improve Student Success.* Retrieved June 14, 2007 from http://www.ccsse.org/publications/CCSSENationalReport2006.pdf

Foundations of Excellence in the First College Year. (2005). *Foundational Dimensions.* Retrieved September 8, 2006, from http://www.fyfoundations.org/

Jenkins, D., Bailey, T.R., Crosta, P., Leinbach, T., Marshall, J., Soonachan, A., and Van Noy, M. (May 2006). *What community college policies and practices are effective in promoting student success? A study of high- and low-impact institutions.* Community College Research Center. New York: Teachers College, Columbia University.

Kuh, G.D., Kinzie, J., Buckley, J.A., Bridges, B.K., and Hayek, J.C. (2007). Piecing together the student success puzzle: Research, propositions, and recommendations. *ASHE Higher Education Report*, 32(5). San Francisco, CA: Jossey-Bass.

Luan, J. (2006). *Impact of tutoring on student success at Cabrillo College.* Unpublished report. Aptos, CA: Cabrillo College.

McClenney, K., Marti, C.N., and Adkins, C. (2007). *Student engagement and student outcomes: Key findings from CCSSE validation research.* [Electronic version]. Retrieved June 13, 2007, from http://www.ccsse.org/.

Pascarella, E. T., and Terenzini, P.T. (2005). *How college affects students* (2nd ed.). San Francisco, CA: Jossey-Bass.

Patton, L.D., Morelon, C., Whitehead, D.M., and Hossler, D. (2006). Campus-based retention initiatives: Does the emperor have clothes? In E.P. St. John and M. Wilkerson (Eds.), *Reframing persistence research to improve academic success. New Directions for Institutional Research*, No. 130. San Francisco: Jossey-Bass.

Purnell, R., and Blank, S. (2004). *Support success: Services that may help low-income students succeed in community college.* New York: MDRC.

Tinto, V. (1987). *Leaving college, rethinking the causes and cures of student attrition.* Chicago, IL: University of Chicago Press.

Washtenaw Community College. (2006). *Tutoring data analysis: Winter 2006 results in comparison with fall 2005 results.* Unpublished paper. Institutional Research Department.

James Kostecki *is senior manager of survey research, American Academy of Dermatology in Schaumburg, Illinois. He can be reached at jkotecki@aad.org.*

Trudy Bers *is executive director of Institutional Research, Curriculum and Strategic Planning at Oakton Community College in Des Plaines, Illinois. She can be reached at tbers@oakton.edu.*

Effects of Learning-Style Responsive Versus Traditional Staff Development on Community College Professors' Attitudes Toward Alternative Instructional Strategies

Christina T. Hart
Indian River Community College

Rita Dunn
Instructional Leadership Doctoral Program
and Center for the Study of Learning and Teaching Styles

How does one know whether traditional or innovative staff development is working? This study compared the effects of professors' attitudes toward learning through traditional staff development versus alternative instructional strategies for teaching community college students. Eight-four professors participated in this study. The average participant was a White female between the ages of 40-49 who taught in the departments of Arts and Sciences. For this study the participants attended workshops focused on three different instructional strategies for teaching college students – Programmed Learning Sequences (PLS), Team Learning (TL), and Circle of Knowledge (COK). These three strategies were taught in a counter-balanced design. Thus, each group of faculty was taught with both a traditional and a learning-style approach, but in a different sequence so that each group served as its own control in a repeated measures design. The Productivity Environmental Preference Survey (PEPS) identified the participants' learning styles. The Semantic Differential Scale (SDS) (Pizzo, 1981) assessed their attitudes toward each of the two different instructional approaches. The community college faculty's attitudes significantly ($p < .05$) favored the learning-styles responsive approach over the traditionally taught workshop regardless of the content.

Introduction

Extensive literature supports the premise that adults learn more, at a faster pace, and retain it to a greater degree with learning-style responsive, rather than traditional staff development sessions. According to Raupers (2000) and Taylor, Dunn, Dunn, Klavas, and Montgomery (1999), to provide effective training, all participants' learning styles should be identified, and responsive instructional approaches should be used to present in-service through each learner's perceptual, processing, and sociological strengths. Both researchers reached that conclusion based on their independent experimental studies with staff development sessions in which certified teachers were exposed to innovative approaches with two distinct strategies—traditional lectures accompanied by PowerPoint presentations and distributed readings versus with learning-style responsive instructional resources.

Raupers' and Taylor's conclusions were corroborated by Boyle and Dolle (2002) and Boyle, Russo, and Lefkowitz (2003) with law school students; by Dunn, Ingham, and Deckinger (1995) with corporate employees; by Ingham (2000) with undergraduate engineering students; and by both Lefkowitz (1998) and Miller (1998a, 1998b) with adults studying allied-health issues. All reported that when professors observed the significantly increased achievement and more positive attitudes among the students in their classes, in contrast with the same professors teaching those same students traditionally, the teachers' awareness of the new techniques changed to interest and approval.

In each of those studies, participants' learning styles were identified with valid and reliable identification instruments. Earlier research by Beaty (1986) indicated that, without a reliable and valid assessment, high school teachers who had taught seniors for a full semester were unable to correctly identify those youths' styles merely by observations. They misinterpreted many behaviors in light of teachers' predispositions to conventional requirements. For example, when students consistently moved in their seats, teachers reported them as "hyperactive" instead of recognizing that many of the males needed informal seating or periodic opportunities for changing their positions. When students could not remember much of what had been said during a lecture, teachers assumed that they were not paying attention. However, the instruments documented that those students were low-auditory, high-kinesthetic learners and should have been taught through, for example, Floor Games.

Researchers have reported that staff development for

community college faculty typically is delivered through lectures or readings by an expert in a particular field and without documented research or practical suggestions for classroom applications (Wood & Thompson, 1993). Furthermore, because community college professors rarely are exposed to innovative practices through either small-group instructional strategies or PLSs, the literature provides little insight concerning their perceptions of whether or not they learn effectively that way—or even might enjoy those processes.

Therefore, one purpose of this research was to compare the effects of traditional versus learning-style responsive staff development to determine the relative impact of each treatment on faculties' attitudes toward the instructional strategies and their content. Another purpose was to determine the extent to which learning-style responsive staff development produced significant differences among participants' attitudes toward alternative approaches to teaching.

Statement of the Problem

More than three decades ago, Knowles (1970) asserted that to learn effectively, adults required environmental conditions that differed from those of high school students. At approximately the same time, Dunn and Dunn (1972) identified the existence of *individual* rather than group adult learning styles. During the past almost four decades, their research revealed that, unlike Knowles' (1970) proposition of a group style, adults varied substantially in how they mastered new and difficult academic knowledge. That finding was corroborated among persons between the ages of 50-80 enrolled in an alternative metropolitan university program (Bovell & Ansalone, 2001), law-school students in legal writing courses (Boyle, 2000; Boyle & Dunn, 1998), allied-health students enrolled in a state medical college (Lefkowitz, 1998), students between the ages of 60-87 housed in a residence facility (Van Wynen, 1998, 2001), and undergraduate students in a Puerto Rican college (Vazquez, 1985).

Other experimental studies documented that adults not only learned differently from each other, but also achieved statistically higher achievement- and attitude-test scores when they were taught with instructional strategies responsive to, rather than dissonant from, their individual learning-style characteristics (Dunn, Ingham, & Deckinger, 1995; Ingham, 1991, 2000; Lenehan, Dunn, Ingham, Murray, and Signer, 1994; Miller, 1998a, 1998b; Miller & Dunn, 1997). Therefore, we hypothesized that participants who received staff development through their learning-style preferences would evidence statistically higher attitudinal test scores than participants who received traditional staff development. This judgment was based on previous findings with school teachers by Hamlin (2002), Raupers (1999), and Taylor (1999).

Beyond the data ascertaining the benefits of learning-style based staff development on the adults taught that way, extensive documentation indicates that students taught by faculty who personally experienced learning-style responsive training achieved statistically higher standardized achievement-test scores (Dunn & DeBello, 1999). Those findings support the belief that learning-style responsive teacher training positively affected the instruction subsequently provided for the students of professors so trained.

Statistical Design

Workshops were provided for all participants using a repeated measures design in which each group experienced both treatments so as to serve as their own control in a counterbalanced sequence. The purpose of the repeated measures design was to provide all participants with both the traditional and the learning-styles treatments. The purpose of the counterbalancing procedure was to deliver the experimental and control treatments in a different sequence to eliminate possible bias because of the sequence in which each treatment was experienced. Miller (1998b) refers to this design procedure as repetitive, multiple, or sequential.

To capitalize on a counterbalanced design, the same two treatments (traditional versus learning styles) were used to teach new instructional strategies, but were reversed for each group. Thus, although each group learned the same instructional content in each session, its participants learned that content through two different instructional strategies—learning styles versus traditional and in two different sequences.

Subjects, Instruments, and Procedures
Subjects

The sample was composed of 84 professors from three Florida community colleges. Participants ranged in age from 22 to more than 69 years. Seventy-four percent were female and twenty-six percent were male. Participants taught community college courses in a variety of disciplines with 63% from Arts and Sciences, 15% from Vocational Education, 12% from Allied Health, and 10 percent from Adult Education. Although we found that the participants represented 83% White, 8% African-American, 6% Hispanic, and 2% Asian/Asian Pacific Islander, the numbers were far too small to generate any type of meaningful conclusion. However, the average participant was a White female, between the ages of 40 and 49 years, who taught in the arts and sciences.

Due to extenuating circumstances beyond the control of the researchers, the sample was limited to volunteers. Four hurricanes that besieged Florida that year prevented others who had planned to attend from participating.

Instruments

The following instruments were administered in this investigation:

The PEPS (Dunn, Dunn, & Price, 1974, 1979, 1981, 1986, 1989, 1990, 1991, 1993, 1996) is a 100-item self-report questionnaire that employs a 5-point Likert scale that ranges on a continuum from strongly disagree to strongly agree to measure the learning-style preferences of adults. The computerized processing of the assessment produces an individual profile that provides scores for 20 learning-style preferences (sound, light, temperature, design, motivation, persistence, responsibility [conformity/ nonconformity], structure, working alone or with peers, needing an authority figure nearby to provide feedback, learning in several ways as opposed to in patterns, perceptual strengths [auditory, visual, tactual or kinesthetic strengths], needing intake while concentrating, and time of day energy levels [i.e., early or late morning, afternoon, or evening, and mobility]).

The T-Hart Achievement Test (THART), a researcher-developed achievement test, was submitted to a jury of three research experts, certified in learning styles and selected based on recommendations from the Learning-Styles Network in New York. These experts examined the THART pretests and posttests to:

(a) Determine that questions actually asked what they were purported to ask,
(b) Determine their appropriateness for use with community college professors, and
(c) Conduct content analyses to assess the comparability of the two learning styles and two traditional contents.

Changes recommended by these experts were made to the instruments prior to the workshops.

These instruments were used as a pretest and posttest assessment consisting of eight multiple-choice questions based on the goals of each of the two staff development workshops, PLS and Small Group Techniques (SGT). An exploratory factor analysis was conducted for both instruments to determine the variance components and the construct validity of each instrument.

The SDS (Pizzo, 1981) is used to compare the community college professors' attitudes toward the two instructional approaches in contrast with each other. The following 12 pairs of bipolar objectives were used in the SDS: Confused-clear minded, energetic-tired, nervous-calm, strong-weak, tense-relaxed, wonderful-terrible, shaky-stead, bad-good, dull-sharp, successful-unsuccessful, and interested-bored. On a scale of one to five, professors rated their comparative feelings toward the two instructional methods using the 12 pairs of words.

Procedures

Professors were invited to participate in a workshop designed to acquaint them with learning-style strategies applicable for teaching community college students. Electronic mail was sent to faculty through each college contact soliciting volunteers. Volunteers were provided with two alternative dates from which to choose to participate in one of the workshops. Both treatments were based on specific learning-style methods—a PLS and two SGT, TL and COK (Dunn & Dunn, 1999). The three strategies were taught in either a traditional or a learning-style responsive treatment. Three weeks prior to the workshop, volunteers were asked to read and respond to a packet of forms that included a letter of explanation, requested demographic data, a consent form, and a PEPS questionnaire.

At each of the three community colleges, participants engaged in a 60-minute workshop focused on learning about the PLS using a learning-style responsive format. Following a 30-minute break for food, the same participants experienced a second, 60-minute workshop about TL and COK using a traditional format. One week later, a second group of participants from the same college engaged in a 60-minute workshop about PLS using a traditional format. Following a 30-minute break for food, the same participants experienced a second 60-minute workshop about TL and COK using a learning-style responsive format.

Two separate workshops were conducted each day, one serving as the experimental treatment (learning-style responsive format) and the other as the control treatment (traditional format). Content consisted of two different learning-style instructional approaches—a PLS and SGT. Groups 1, 3, 5, and 7 experienced their first workshop using a learning-style responsive treatment with content focused on PLS.

Following a break, the same groups experienced a second workshop using a traditional treatment with content focused on SGT. Groups 2, 4, 6, and 8 first experienced a workshop using a traditional treatment with content focused on PLS; and, after a break, the same groups experienced a second workshop using a learning-styles responsive treatment with content focused on SGT.

Each treatment was preceded by an achievement pretest and concluded with both an achievement posttest and an attitudinal posttest. Each group acted as its own control with the treatments offered to each group reversed on subsequent sessions to afford counterbalancing. Each group learned new content through two different instructional strategies, traditional versus learning styles, in two different sequences.

Procedures Specific to the Learning-Style Responsive Workshops

Participants in the learning-style responsive workshops were given their learning-style profiles based on the PEPS and received an explanation of their own learning-style profiles. They then were invited to choose anywhere in the room to work where they felt comfortable. They were advised that they could move about to complete the workshop objectives in a variety of ways—depending on their identified learning-style preferences. They could master the objectives concerned with the PLS or the SGT tactually by using Task Cards, a Flip Chute, a Pic-A-Hole, a PLS, or an Electroboard. As an alternative, if they preferred, they were invited to complete the objectives using a kinesthetic Floor Game or a TL exercise, either alone, in pairs, or in a small group of three or four. They also were free to learn or review via a series of overhead transparencies or selected readings.

For those whose PEPS results indicated the need for an informal design, the room included cushions on the floor. A rocking chair was provided for those with a preference for movement. Snacks and drinks were available for the faculty whose styles indicated the need for intake. Desk lamps were available for those who preferred bright illumination, and instructional audio tapes and tape recorders were available for auditory learners. A CD player with instrumental music and headphones was available for those who preferred sound while learning.

Procedures Specific to the Traditional Workshops

Participants in the traditional workshops sat in traditional desks facing the front of the room and listened to the researcher lecture on the content objectives with accompanying overhead transparencies. Participants also read aloud from selected readings related to the content objectives.

Following both the traditional treatment and the learning-style responsive treatment, the researcher-developed posttest, THART, was administered to ascertain the participants' knowledge of the workshop objectives. The SDS (Pizzo, 1981) was then administered to assess the participants' attitude toward the workshop.

Data Analysis

Descriptive statistics were generated on all variables relevant to the research question. Analyses were conducted to determine if the distributions for each variable met the assumptions of parametric statistical methodology—homogeneity of variance, linearity, normality, and independence. Primary analysis was conducted to test the hypothesis relative to the research question using a t-test of correlated samples and an Analysis of Covariance (ANCOVA) of the independent samples (experimental and control) using the pretest as the covariate. The mean, standard deviation, and t-tests of the PEPS scores for the traditional and experimental subjects revealed significant differences among their learning-style preferences. Participants were made aware of their individual learning-style traits and encouraged to capitalize on them during the experimental sessions by using resources that we provided such as multi-sensory materials and environmental props—cushions and rocking chairs for those who needed an informal environment, desk lamps and headphones for those who needed acoustical or illumination variance, and snacks for those who needed intake.

The SDS (Pizzo, 1981) assessed participants' attitudes toward instructional methods. Means and t-test scores for each scale revealed faculty attitudes and comfort levels when receiving learning-styles staff development through their preferences compared to when they received traditional lecture-type instruction. Secondary analyses were conducted to test the relationships among PEPS variables and the SDS. Using a backward linear regression technique a parsimonious model of significant variables was developed.

Findings

Participants receiving staff development through their learning-style preferences evidenced statistically higher attitudinal test scores than participants who received traditional staff development, corroborating previous reports by Hamlin (2002), Raupers (1999), and Taylor (1999). Participants reported a statistically more positive attitude within each group following the learning-styles responsive experimental treatment regardless of the content—PLS, TL or COK—as demonstrated through the paired samples test in Table 1.

Within groups, a difference in attitudes was found to be significant

Table 1. Paired Samples Test – Attitude

Pair	Mean	SD	Std. Err. Mean	Sig. (2-tailed)
A1 – B2	2.50	8.343	1.258	.053
B1 – A2	4.52	9.310	1.597	.008

at the p <.05 level when the experimental group experienced the learning-style responsive treatment when learning about the PLS, and at the p <.008 level when the experimental group experienced the learning-style responsive treatment when learning about the TL and COK. Between groups, a difference in attitude was found to be significant at the p <.036 level when the experimental group experienced the learning-style responsive treatment when learning about the PLS and at the p <.023 level when the experimental group experienced the learning-style responsive treatment when learning about the TL and COK.

Concerned with whether or not a significant relationship existed between the participants' learning-style preferences as measured by the PEPS and their attitudinal scores as measured by the SDS following the two treatments, a regression analysis was conducted using a backward method for removing variables from the model. A significant model would suggest that an explanatory linear relationship existed between the variables in the model that may have had some substantive meaningful application. The most parsimonious model is considered the best model because it is the easiest and most practical to implement in real life with variables that are correlated and meaningful. It answers the practical questions of, "Does attitude make a difference when learning?"

The first model test examined the outcomes of the treatments using Content 2, SGT as the dependent variable. Using the backward method, all the potential variables initially were included because, to best explain potential outcomes using Content 2, SGT, the explanatory variable was unknown. Running the model should have indicated the models that produced the most efficient R square. All learning-style variables and the attitude variable were included in the equation to determine which PEPS variables impacted outcomes, whether the attitudinal variable truly explained outcomes when using Content 2, and which variables were best correlated with the outcome variable to the achievement score and SGT.

The first model developed indicated that it had eight distinct variables for explaining outcomes derived from utilizing Content 2 (SGT). In Table 2, that model produced an R square = .519 or 52% of the variance accounted for with this data model. Modeling deleted those variables that were less significant.

In Table 3, all models were produced because all were significant. There were five significant models, but only one was parsimonious as evidenced by how the R changed when the variables dropped out. There were four variables that explained significantly the impact of learning using SGT. The parsimonious model showed the greatest significance producing an R square of 48%. Almost 50% of the variance of the outcome of using SGT could be explained using this linear combination. The qualities of variety, needing motivation, learning alone or with peers,; and the sense of responsibility were all important.

Using the beta weight (instead of B weight), every one was significant. B weight is related to using raw scores in the model and is a coefficient. The model would be the SGT performance score. Taking the B weight equal to that minus 0.1 (times the motivation score that emanated from the PEPS), plus .06 for the responsibility variable, plus the .04 alone/peer, plus .09 need for variety, clearly indicated this is an explanatory model, not a predictive model.

In Table 4, the weighting showed how important it was and the standardized coefficients or weights—61%, 53%, 43%, 58%—were negative because the motivation variable was an important factor in the effect of SGT. Of the three noted here, motivation and needing variety were the two most highly weighted factors—motivated, .616, and needing variety, .580, for SGT. Table 4 reflects the coefficients for each of the five models and only the fifth model was parsimonious.

Table 2. Small-Group Technique Model Summary

Model	R Treatment2=E (Selected)	R Square	Adjusted R Square	Std. Error of the Estimate	R Square Change	F Change	df1	df2	Sig. F Change
1	.721[a]	.519	.327	.679	.519	2.701	8	20	.034
2	.721[b]	.519	.359	.663	.000	.005	1	20	.944
3	.720[c]	.518	.386	.648	-.001	.063	1	21	.804
4	.715[d]	.511	.404	.639	-.007	.320	1	22	.577
5	.696[e]	.485	.399	.641	-.026	1.204	1	23	.284

a. Predictors: (Constant), Variety, Attitude-SGT, Motivation, Authority, Structure, Alone/Peer, Responsible, Persistent
b. Predictors: (Constant), Variety, Motivation, Authority, Structure, Alone/Peer, Responsible, Persistent
c. Predictors: (Constant), Variety, Motivation, Structure, Alone/Peer, Responsible, Persistent
d. Predictors: (Constant), Variety, Motivation, Structure, Alone/Peer, Responsible
e. Predictors: (Constant), Variety, Motivation, Alone/Peer, Responsible

The same applied to the PLS. The PLS was running 11 models. The R square indicated that, of the 11 models, the only one that was significant was the 11th model that was somewhat significant at the .05 level and was, therefore, the parsimonious model. Structure at -.328 was the highest weighted predictive factor for PLS. These findings merely corroborated previous data generated by utilization of PLS treatments with a variety of experimental studies with students at elementary through professional levels (Dunn & Griggs, 2003). A PLS works well with those whose learning-style profile indicates a preference for structure, visual input and tactile stimulation (Dunn & Dunn, 1993).

Summary and Discussion

Participants reported statistically more positive attitudes toward the learning-styles experimental treatments regardless of the treatment and the content—PLS or SGT (TL and COK), as demonstrated through the paired samples test in Table 1. Those who initially participated reluctantly were noticeably engaged by the end of the experimental workshops. This observation was supported by their attitudinal-test scores.

During the workshops, participants were noticeably more animated and engaged while using the learning-style responsive strategies than while using the traditional format. Following each workshop, participants expressed their enthusiasm for what they had experienced during the learning-style treatments and indicated their interest in learning additional strategies for teaching their own college classes.

Extensive data support significant differences in how adults acquire, process, internalize, and retain new and difficult information (Dunn & Griggs, 2003). Staff developers need to make these differences central to teaching and learning and should not permit group presentations to be taught uniformly. Because professional development is key to instructional improvement, knowledge about adults' varied styles should serve as the basis for planning and implementing workshops and other types of presentations (Wood & Thompson, 1993).

National emphasis is currently on the need to improve the quality of college teaching (Rochford, 2004). Many researchers have shown that teaching students through their individual learning styles is more effective than teaching them traditionally (Boyle & Dolle, 2002; Boyle, Russo, & Lefkowitz, 2003; Dunn & Griggs, 2003). This is the first study to demonstrate that learning-style in-service is better received than traditional teaching by community college professors. As this study used only 84 faculty members under trying conditions (i.e., weather storms), it is important to identify many unknowns that could be confounding the results.

Future researchers should replicate this study to determine whether learning-style strategies are equally as appealing to senior college faculty regardless of content and, subsequently, how this type of learning continues to impact the next generation of learners attending institutions of higher education. A counter-balanced design of this format using students from different programs (e.g., English majors versus nursing majors) also may lend itself to more in-depth conclusions on learning style and teaching methods. If faculty members are not able to administer a learning-styles inventory or go to such great lengths as to counter balance the treatment, then faculty should consider providing at least two different

Table 3. Small Group Technique Model-ANOVA

Model		Sum of Squares	df	Mean Square	F	Sig.
1	Regression	9.956	8	1.245	2.701	.034[a]
	Residual	9.216	20	.461		
	Total	19.172	28			
2	Regression	9.954	7	1.422	3.239	.017[b]
	Residual	9.218	21	.439		
	Total	19.172	28			
3	Regression	9.926	6	1.654	3.936	.008[c]
	Residual	9.246	22	.420		
	Total	19.172	28			
4	Regression	9.792	5	1.958	4.802	.004[d]
	Residual	9.381	23	.408		
	Total	19.172	28			
5	Regression	9.301	5	1.958	4.802	.004[e]
	Residual	9.872	24	.411		
	Total	19.172	28			

a. Predictors: (Constant), Variety, Attitude-SGT, Motivation, Authority, Structure, Alone/Peer, Respons Persistent
b. Predictors: (Constant), Variety, Motivation, Authority, Structure, Alone/Peer, Responsible, Persister
c. Predictors: (Constant), Variety, Motivation, Structure, Alone/Peer, Responsible, Persistent
d. Predictors: (Constant), Variety, Motivation, Structure, Alone/Peer, Responsible
e. Predictors: (Constant), Variety, Motivation, Alone/Peer, Responsible
f. Dependent Variable: SGI-IIA-IIB THART post-test/8
g. Selecting only cases for which Treatment 2 = E

learning-style strategies per module. They also should empower students to evaluate the effectiveness of each strategy and to use these same approaches at home. This may encourage students to become lifelong learners.

References

Beaty, S. A. (1986). The effect of in-service training on the ability of teachers to observe learning styles of students (Doctoral dissertation, Oregon State University, 1986). *Dissertation Abstracts International, 46*(06), 1998A.

Bovell, C., & Ansalone, G. E. (2001). An exploration of adult learning style: Doesn't everyone learn similarly? *Michigan Community College Journal, 7*(2), 41-59.

Boyle, R. A. (2000). Bringing learning-style instructional strategies to law schools: You be the judge! In R. Dunn & S. A. Griggs (Eds.), *Practical approaches to using learning styles in higher education* (pp. 155-165). Westport, CT: Bergin & Garvey.

Boyle, R. A., & Dolle, L. (2002). Providing structure to law students—introducing the Programmed Learning Sequence as an instructional tool. *Journal of the Legal Writing Institute, 8*, 59-146.

Boyle, R., & Dunn, R. (1998). Teaching law students through individual learning styles. *Albany Law Review, 62*(1), 213-255.

Boyle, R. A., Russo, K., & Lefkowitz, R. F. (2003). Presenting a new instructional tool for teaching law-related courses: A contract activity package for motivated and independent learners. *Gonzaga Law Review, 38*(1), 1-31.

Dunn, R., Ingham, J., & Deckinger, L. (1995). Effects of matching and mismatching corporate employees' perceptual preferences and instructional strategies on training achievement and attitudes. *Journal of Applied Business Research, 11*(3), 30-37.

Dunn, R., & DeBello, T.C. (Eds.) (1999). *Improved test scores, attitudes, and behaviors in America's schools: Supervisors' success stories.* Westport, CT: Bergin & Garvey.

Dunn, R., & Dunn, K. (1972). *Practical approaches to individualizing instruction: Contracts and other effective teaching strategies.* Englewood Cliffs, NJ. Parker Publishing Division of Prentice Hall, 21-28.

Dunn, R., & Dunn, K. (1999). *The complete guide to the learning styles in-service system.* Boston, MA: Allyn & Bacon.

Dunn, R., Dunn, K., & Price, G. E. (1974, 1979, 1981, 1986, 1989, 1990, 1991, 1993, 1996). *Learning style inventor.* Lawrence, KS: Price Systems.

Dunn, R. & Griggs, S.A. (2003). Synthesis of the Dunn and Dunn learning style model research: Who, what, when, where, and so what? Jamaica, NY: St. John's University, Center for the Study of Learning and Teaching Styles.

Dunn, R., Ingham, J., & Deckinger, L. (1995). Effects of matching and mismatching corporate employees' perceptual preferences and instructional strategies on training achievement and attitudes. *Journal of Applied Business Research, 11*(3), 30-37.

Hamlin, T. (2002). Effects of learning-style strategies and metacognition on adults' achievement. *National Forum of Applied Educational Research Journal, 15* (2), 3-17.

Ingham, J. M. (1991). The 'sense-able' choice: Matching instruction with employee perceptual preference significantly increases training effectiveness. *Human Resource Development Quarterly, 2*(1), 53-64.

Ingham, J. (2000). Meeting the academic challenges of an undergraduate engineering curriculum. In R. Dunn & S. A. Griggs (Eds.), *Practical approaches to using learning styles in higher education* (pp. 166-173). Westport, CT: Bergin & Garvey.

Knowles, M. S. (1970). *The modern practice of adult education: Andragogy versus pedagogy.* New York, NY: Association Press.

Lefkowitz, R. F. (1998). Teaching health information management

Table 4. Small-Group Technique Model Coefficients

Model		Unstandardized Coefficients B	Std. Error	Standardized Coefficients Beta	t	Sig.
1	(Constant)	3.907	3.917		.997	.330
	Attitude - SGT	.001	.021	.012	.071	.944
	Motivation	-.101	.035	-.647	-2.891	.009
	Persistent	.020	.042	.105	.484	.634
	Responsible	.049	.022	.463	2.251	.036
	Structure	-.023	.023	-.220	-1.006	.327
	Alone/Peer	.034	.016	.402	2.149	.044
	Authority	-.005	.021	-.042	-.242	.811
	Variety	.101	.036	.626	2.758	.012
2	(Constant)	4.022	3.477		1.157	.260
	Motivation	-.101	.033	-.644	-3.017	.007
	Persistent	.019	.039	.101	.494	.626
	Responsible	.049	.021	.463	2.306	.031
	Structure	-.023	.021	-.215	-1.066	.299
	Alone/Peer	.033	.015	.399	2.250	.035
	Authority	-.005	.020	-.043	-.252	.804
	Variety	.100	.034	.621	2.925	.008
3	(Constant)	3.529	2.811		1.255	.223
	Motivation	-.101	.033	-.645	-3.089	.005
	Persistent	.021	.038	.111	.566	.577
	Responsible	.049	.021	.464	2.362	.027
	Structure	-.024	.020	-.230	-1.218	.236
	Alone/Peer	.034	.014	.407	2.392	.026
	Variety	.103	.031	.642	3.350	.003
4	(Constant)	4.274	2.447		1.747	.094
	Motivation	-.092	.028	-.589	-3.248	.004
	Responsible	.050	.020	.468	2.417	.024
	Structure	-.020	.018	-.186	-1.097	.284
	Alone/Peer	.034	.014	.408	2.433	.023
	Variety	.096	.028	.598	3.467	.002
5	(Constant)	3.001	2.163		1.387	-.178
	Motivation	-.096	.028	-.616	-3.417	.002
	Responsible	.056	.020	.533	2.883	.008
	Alone/Peer	.039	.014	.461	2.861	.009
	Variety	.093	.028	.580	3.362	.003

a. Dependent Variable: SGI-IIA-IIB THART post-test/8
b. Selecting only cases for which Treatment 2 = E

Lenehan, M. C., Dunn, R., Ingham, J., Murray, J., & Signer, B. (1994). Effects of learning-style intervention on college students' achievement, anxiety, anger, and curiosity. *Journal of College Student Development, 35*, 461-466.

Miller, J. A. (1998a). Enhancement of achievement and attitudes through individualized learning-style presentations of two allied health courses. *Journal of Allied Health, 27*, 150-156.

Miller, J. A. (1998b). Teaching baccalaureate diagnostic medical sonography students with a learning-style approach. In R. Dunn & S. A. Griggs (Eds.), *Learning styles and the nursing profession* (pp. 65-79). New York, NY: National League for Nursing.

Miller, J. A., & Dunn, R. (1997). The use of learning styles in sonography education. *Journal of Diagnostic Medical Sonography, 13*, 304-308.

Pizzo, J. (1981). An investigation of the relationship between selected acoustic environments and sound, an element of learning style, as they affect sixth-grade students' reading achievement and attitudes (Doctoral dissertation, St. John's University, 1981). *Dissertation Abstracts International, 42*(06), 2475A.

Raupers, P. M. (1999). Effects of accommodating perceptual learning-style preferences on long-term retention and attitudes toward technology of elementary and secondary teachers in professional development training (Doctoral dissertation, St. John's University, 1999). *Dissertation Abstracts International, 59*(11), 4031A.

Raupers, P. M. (2000). Effects of accommodating learning-style preferences on long-term retention of technology training content. *National Forum of Applied Educational Research Journal, 13*(2), 23-26.

Rochford, R. A. (2004). Improving academic performance and retention among remedial students. *Community College Enterprise, 10*(2), 23-26.

Taylor, R. G. (1999). Effects of learning-style responsive versus traditional staff development on the knowledge and attitudes of urban and suburban elementary school teachers. (Doctoral dissertation, St. John's University, 1999). *Dissertation Abstracts International, 60*(04), 1089A.

Taylor, R. G., Dunn, R., Dunn, K. J., Klavas, A., & Montgomery, N. (1999). Effects of learning-style responsive versus traditional staff development on the knowledge and attitudes of teachers. *National Forum of Applied Educational Research Journal, 13*(1), 63-75.

Van Wynen, E. A. (1998). How do you think? Two sides to every story. In R. Dunn & S. A. Griggs (Eds.), *Learning styles and the nursing profession* (pp. 41-52). New York, New York: National League for Nursing.

Table 5. Programmed Learning Sequence Model Summary

Model	R Treatment=E (Selected)	R Square	Adjusted R Square	Std. Error of the Estimate	R Square Change	F Change	df1	df2	Sig. F Change
1	.490[a]	.240	-.048	.853	.240	.832	11	29	.611
2	.487[b]	.237	-.017	.840	-.002	.095	1	29	.760
3	.481[c]	.231	.008	.830	-.006	.234	1	30	.632
4	.477[d]	.227	.034	.819	-.004	.171	1	31	.682
5	.469[e]	.220	.055	.810	-.007	.290	1	32	.594
6	.454f	.206	.066	.805	-.014	.607	1	33	.441
7	.431[g]	.186	.069	.804	-.020	.863	1	34	.359
8	.407[h]	.166	.073	.802	-.020	.864	1	35	.359
9	.383[i]	.146	.077	.800	-.019	.828	1	36	.369
10	.370[j]	.137	.091	.794	-.010	.413	1	37	.524
11	.328[k]	.108	.085	.797	-.029	1.284	1	38	.264

a. Predictors: (Constant), Kinesthetic, Attitude-PLS-TRAD, Responsible, Alone/Peer, Auditory, Visual, Structure, Persistent, Design, Tactile, Motivation
b. Predictors: (Constant), Kinesthetic, Attitude-PLS-TRAD, Responsible, Alone/Peer, Auditory, Visual, Structure, Design, Tactile, Motivation
c. Predictors: (Constant), Kinesthetic, Responsible, Alone/Peer, Auditory, Visual, Structure, Design, Tactile, Motivation
d. Predictors: (Constant), Kinesthetic, Responsible, Alone/Peer, Auditory, Visual, Structure, Tactile, Motivation
e. Predictors: (Constant), Responsible, Alone/Peer, Auditory, Visual, Structure, Tactile, Motivation
f. Predictors: (Constant), Responsible, Alone/Peer, Visual, Structure, Tactile, Motivation
h. Predictors: (Constant), Alone/Peer, Visual, Structure, Tactile
i. Predictors: (Constant), Visual, Structure, Tactile
j. Predictors: (Constant), Visual, Structure
k. Predictors: (Constant), Structure

Van Wynen, E. A. (2001) A key to successful aging: Learning-style patterns of older adults. *Journal of Gerontological Nursing, 29*(9) pp. 6-15.

Vazquez, A. W. (1985). Description of learning styles of high-risk adult students taking evening courses in urban community colleges in Puerto Rico. (Doctoral dissertation, The Union for Experimenting Colleges and Universities, 1986). *Dissertation Abstracts International, 47*(04), 1157A.

Wood, F. W., & S. R. Thompson (1993). Assumptions about staff development based on research and best practice. *Journal of Staff Development* 14(4): 52-56.

Christina T. Hart, Ph.D. *is associate vice president of Institutional Effectiveness at Indian River Community College, Fort Pierce, Florida. She can be reached at Indian River Community College, Main Campus, 3209 Virginia Avenue, Fort Pierce, FL 34981-5596; by phone: (772) 462-4703 ; by email: chart@ircc.edu*

Rita Dunn, Ed.D. *is professor and coordinator of the Instructional Leadership Doctoral Program and director of the Center for the Study of Learning and Teaching Styles, St. John's University, New York. She can be reached at St. John's University, 8000 Utopia Parkway Queens, New York 11439; by phone: (718) 990-6336; by email: rdunn241@msn.com*

Table 6. Programmed Learning Sequence Model-ANOVA

Model		Sum of Squares	df	Mean Square	F	Sig.
1	Regression	6.657	11	.605	.832	.611[a]
	Residual	21.099	29	.728		
	Total	27.756	40			
2	Regression	6.588	10	.659	.934	.517[b]
	Residual	21.168	30	.706		
	Total	27.456	40			
3	Regression	6.423	9	.714	1.037	.434[c]
	Residual	21.333	31	.688		
	Total	27.756	40			
4	Regression	6.305	8	.788	1.176	.344[d]
	Residual	21.451	32	.670		
	Total	27.756	40			
5	Regression	6.111	7	.873	1.331	.267[e]
	Residual	21.646	33	.656		
	Total	27.756	40			
6	Regression	5.712	6	.952	1.468	.218[f]
	Residual	22.044	34	.648		
	Total	27.756	40			
7	Regression	5.152	5	1.030	1.596	.187[g]
	Residual	22.604	35	.645		
	Total	27.756	40			
8	Regression	4.594	4	1.149	1.785	.153[h]
	Residual	23.162	36	.643		
	Total	27.756	40			
9	Regression	4.061	3	1.354	2.114	.115[i]
	Residual	23.695	37	.640		
	Total	27.756	40			
10	Regression	3.797	2	1.898	3.011	.061[j]
	Residual	23.959	38	.631		
	Total	27.756	40			
11	Regression	2.987	1	2.987	4.704	.036[k]
	Residual	24.769	39	.635		
	Total	27.756	40			

a. Predictors: (Constant), Kinesthetic, Attitude-PLS-TRAD, Responsible, Alone/Peer, Auditory, Visual, Structure, Persistent, Design, Tactile, Motivation
b. Predictors: (Constant), Kinesthetic, Attitude-PLS-TRAD, Responsible, Alone/Peer, Auditory, Visual, Structure, Design, Tactile, Motivation
c. Predictors: (Constant), Kinesthetic, Responsible, Alone/Peer, Auditory, Visual, Structure, Design, Tactile Motivation
d. Predictors: (Constant), Kinesthetic, Responsible, Alone/Peer, Auditory, Visual, Structure, Tactile, Motivation
e. Predictors: (Constant), Responsible, Alone/Peer, Auditory, Visual, Structure, Tactile, Motivation
f. Predictors: (Constant), Responsible, Alone/Peer, Visual, Structure, Tactile, Motivation
h. Predictors: (Constant), Alone/Peer, Visual, Structure, Tactile
i. Predictors: (Constant), Visual, Structure, Tactile
j. Predictors: (Constant), Visual, Structure
k. Predictors: (Constant), Structure

Application of Survival Analysis to Study Timing and Probability of Outcome Attainment by a Community College Student Cohort

Roger Mourad & Ji-Hee Hong
Washtenaw Community College

This study applies competing risks survival analysis to describe outcome attainment for an entire cohort of students who first attended a Midwestern community college in the Fall Semester 2001. Outcome attainment included transfer to a four-year institution, degree/certificate attainment from the community college under study, and transfer to a different two-year college. The analysis also shows how the technique can be used to categorize students who have not realized a graduation or transfer outcome. Outcome probability at different points in time (13 semesters) is calculated and discussed. The effects of demographic and academic variables on timing and type of outcome attained are also discussed. Findings from the study show that outcome attainment was widely distributed over chronological time, there were three discernable stages of outcome attainment across number of semesters enrolled, and cumulative grade point average (GPA) was the most prominent effect on outcome.

Introduction

Community colleges serve a majority of postsecondary students in the United States. The need for community colleges to demonstrate their effectiveness in terms of quantifiable outcomes continues to be a fundamental expectation of policymakers and the public. However, understanding outcome attainment is often difficult for many reasons. Among these reasons, limited access to enrollment records at institutions other than the institution under study, long and irregular enrollment histories, and unapparent student intentions can impede a comprehensive and accurate representation of outcomes.

One issue in studying student outcomes pertaining to community colleges is the fact that, unlike four-year institutions, student goal is often something other than degree attainment. Common goal categories are transfer to a four-year institution (with or without degree/certificate attainment at the two-year institution), education for discrete skill acquisition, or education for personal interest without degree or transfer intent.

A second research problem involved in studying student histories that is especially applicable in the community college context is the phenomenon of stopout. The standard retention model for higher education is based on the traditional four-year university in which a student enrolls and persists from term to term at the same institution until graduating, and this remains the predominant paradigm for the structure of federal and state reporting and research studies. Yet it is very common for enrollment behavior to vary from this model, especially for students who attend community colleges (Adelman, 2005), which raises the issue of how to summarize cohort behavior for students who have not (yet) attained transfer or graduation outcomes and who were not currently enrolled at the time of the study. A related concern is also noted by Voorhees, Smith, and Luan (2006), who cite the need to study the complex array of community college student transitions.

The purpose of this study is to explore the application of survival analysis to enhance the representation of outcomes in the context of community colleges. The potential merit of this method is particularly relevant to community colleges because of the multiplicity of student outcomes, variety of enrollment patterns, and diversity of community college students. Survival analysis models the status of subjects at discrete time points in a way that accounts for changes in the underlying number of subjects who could realize outcomes at different stages. For this reason, it may provide a richer narrative of enrollment and outcomes than a simple representation that is limited to calculating outcomes as a percentage of the number of students who are present at the beginning of a study period.

To our knowledge there is no existing published research that applies survival analysis for the primary purpose of understanding the paths to outcome attainment of entire student cohorts over time from a single community college, and that is the distinct focus of this paper. Since this effort is exploratory, the primary research questions are: What does a study of outcome attainment of community college students look like if it is modeled using survival analysis? How do the results of this application enhance our understanding of the movement of community college students over time?

Study Background

Survival analysis has been used to characterize how enrollment ends and when attrition occurs at four-year institutions (Ronco, 1996; Desjardins 2003). The competing risk technique in survival analysis can be useful because it is designed to address situations in which the individuals under study are at risk of experiencing mutually exclusive events (Singer & Willett, 1991). The value of this method is that it accounts for changes in cohort membership over time and, in particular, provides a means of characterizing students who have not realized an outcome at a certain point but may do so at a later point. In this paper, Cox regression is utilized to conduct a competing risk analysis by measuring the effect of independent variables on the timing of attainment by type of outcome.

Transfer to four-year institutions is a crucial factor in assessing the effectiveness of community colleges because it is a common student goal. Since valid and complete transfer data have not been readily available until recently, the ability of community college researchers to fully account for outcome attainment of their students was not possible in earlier years. Now, however, the National Student Clearinghouse (NSC) maintains student enrollment records for the vast majority of two- and four-year institutions nationally (Porter, 2002), and this study uses NSC enrollment records to capture transfer information for students in the study cohort.

Methodology

The focus of this article is on 3,219 students whose first enrollment record at Washtenaw Community College (WCC) was the Fall Semester 2001. By "first enrollment" we mean the first semester in which the student had a credit course grade record in the college's institutional record system. Use of the term "semester enrolled" in this paper means that the student had a grade record for at least one WCC credit course in the associated semester. A grade record can be a course withdrawal. In contrast, NSC records used in this study to identify enrollment at other institutions are enrollment records, which are often reported before the end of the semester. They can include students who dropped out later in the semester and may not have received a grade, including a course withdrawal.

Note that we included all students whose first term of enrollment at WCC was Fall 2001 regardless of goal, because students often change their goal without documenting it and we wanted to examine outcome attainment for an entire cohort of new students. The endpoint of the period under study was Fall 2005. A total of 13 semesters is covered in this period, including fall, winter, and spring/summer semesters. The sources of the raw data were WCC student records augmented with NSC data (for enrollment at other colleges).

At the outset, it is important to make clear our usage of terms. Herein, the phrase *student outcome* shall mean (a) graduation from the community college, (b) transfer to a four-year college or university, (c) transfer to a different two-year college, or (d) stopout. If a student graduated from WCC and transferred to a four-year college, he or she was categorized as a WCC graduate or four-year transfer, depending on which outcome occurred first. If and when a student attained either outcome, the student was no longer tracked. Students who were enrolled at both a two-year and a four-year school after leaving WCC were classified as four-year transfers. Students who did not graduate from WCC and whose only college enrollment other than WCC was at another community college were categorized as two-year transfers. Students who were still enrolled at WCC in Fall 2005 were designated as current enrollees. Students who did not fit into any of the other categories were designated as stopouts. Outcomes (a), (b), and (c) are considered *formal academic* outcomes; outcome (d) enables us to describe cohort members who may achieve a transfer or graduation outcome at a later date.

By outcome *attainment* we mean the realization of outcomes as defined above, which are mutually exclusive and exhaustive events. The idea of an outcome implies that a fundamental change of state or condition has occurred. It is also important not to equate change of state with realization of an endpoint, particularly with regard to transfer, since graduation may be an ultimate endpoint at another institution but is beyond the scope of this study.

Within the definition of outcome attainment we want to characterize and analyze an entire cohort in terms of outcomes achieved over time based on complete records. To do so, we chose to limit ourselves to data categories that are available for each member of the cohort and that are independently verifiable from institutional records. We are not addressing outcomes that are difficult to measure definitively on a large scale, such as enhancement of job skills and personal growth.

Further, since this is an exploratory study, we have elected to assign "stopout" rather than "dropout" status as a category to define students who (1) have not realized a *formal academic* outcome by the endpoint of the study, and (2) are not enrolled at WCC at the endpoint of the study. This enables us to account for all students in terms of outcomes, including those students who at the endpoint of the period under study have not realized a graduation or transfer outcome but who could do so in the future. We also determined that it would be preferable to distinguish these individuals from students who remained enrolled at the study endpoint. The latter can be considered to have rendered more manifest an intention to continue their studies on the basis that they were enrolled at the latest possible juncture. These students have not yet experienced a change of state or condition represented by graduation, transfer, or stopout.

As shown in Table 1, at the endpoint of the study period, which consisted of 13 consecutive semesters, the largest number of academic outcomes by far was transfer to a four-year university or college. A total of 801 students (25%) transferred to a four-year institution. Less than half that number, 376 students or 12% of the total cohort, ended their association by graduation, while 9% transferred to another two-year college only. About half of the cohort (49% stopped out and 5% of the students were still enrolled at WCC at the endpoint of the study.

The information contained in Table 1 is valuable for the purpose of showing the degree of outcome attainment by members of the cohort at the end of the 13 semesters. However, it does not tell us anything about the character of outcome attainment *within* the 13-semester period or the distribution of outcome attainment based on *when* the outcomes were attained.

One could show the distribution of outcome attainment by simply counting the number of outcomes attained at the conclusion of each term and calculating the percentage of the total starting cohort that the counts represent. While such a breakdown by term does provide basic information about the magnitude of outcome attainment by term across the 13-semester period, it does not tell us anything about the *probability* of outcome occurrence at each period of time.

The key limitation here is that the percentage calculation at each point does not account for the change in status of those cases that attained an outcome prior to each point. For reason of this limitation, the distribution does not provide a representation of outcome attainment that is actually *possible* at each point. Yet since time is the essence of a longitudinal study, representing what is possible at each point is important. Hazard rate serves as a lens for summarizing the trajectory of cohorts toward outcome attainment at different points.

Hazard Rate and Enrollment Patterns

The hazard function is used in survival analysis to summarize the probability of event occurrence at each period of time. The value of this concept is that it provides a way of representing the probability a student will realize a change in outcome by type at different periods. In usual survival analysis terminology, this probability is referred to as a "hazard rate" (reflecting the origin of the method in medical studies to assess risk of death). The hazard rates shown in Table 2 represent the probability that an individual who had enrolled a given number of semesters would realize the outcome after exactly that number of semesters.

The hazard rate, or probability of realizing a particular outcome, was computed as the number of students who fell in an outcome category after x semesters divided by the total number of students who had completed *at least* x semesters. The scale is thus 0.00 to 1.00. For example, there were 2,373 students out of the original 3,219 who had enrolled at WCC in at least two semesters. For members of this group, there was a .154 probability that they stopped out, about half of that probability that they had transferred to a four-year institution (.079), and a much smaller probability of graduation from WCC after two semesters of enrollment at WCC (.008). The unique value of the hazard rate statistic in this context is that for any time period the probability of each

Table 1. Outcome Status After 13 Consecutive Semesters of Time

Outcome	n	%
Transfer to four-year university or college	801	25
Graduation from WCC	376	12
Transfer to two-year college	276	9
Enrolled at WCC	173	5
Stopped attending WCC	1,593	49

Students (*N* = 3,219)

Table 2. Probability of Outcome by Number of Semesters Enrolled

Semesters Enrolled	Students	Stopout n	Stopout Hazard Rate	2-Year Transfer n	2-Year Transfer Hazard Rate	4-Year Transfer n	4-Year Transfer Hazard Rate	WCC Graduate n	WCC Graduate Hazard Rate
1	3,219	534	0.166	94	0.029	201	0.062	17	0.005
2	2,373	365	0.154	64	0.027	187	0.079	19	0.008
3	1,738	206	0.119	34	0.020	86	0.049	17	0.010
4	1,395	152	0.109	34	0.024	89	0.064	28	0.020
5	1,092	102	0.093	19	0.017	70	0.064	33	0.030
6	868	84	0.097	10	0.012	60	0.069	52	0.060
7	662	67	0.101	11	0.017	45	0.068	43	0.065
8	496	42	0.085	7	0.014	26	0.052	45	0.091
9	376	19	0.051	3	0.008	20	0.053	45	0.120
10	289	13	0.045	-	-	10	0.035	31	0.107
11	235	6	0.026	-	-	4	0.017	23	0.098
12	202	0	0.000	-	-	3	0.015	12	0.059
13	187*	3	0.016	-	-	-	-	11	0.059

*173 of the 187 students enrolled for 13 semesters did not realize an outcome and remained enrolled at WCC.

outcome is calculated based solely on the students who have yet to realize an outcome to that point. It achieves this by excluding from the calculation those students who realized outcomes prior to the period.

The probability (hazard rate) of falling into an outcome category after each additional semester increment is plotted in Figure 1. From this depiction, we can see that the probability of graduating from WCC steadily increases with the increase in number of terms enrolled to nine semesters and quickly declines thereafter. In contrast, the probability of transfer to a four-year institution is highest after two semesters at WCC, declines sharply after three semesters, and then flattens until eight semesters of enrollment at WCC, before declining to almost zero for students who attended eleven semesters. The probability of stopout is highest after one semester and generally declines with each incremental increase in semesters enrolled. The probability of two-year transfer is more consistent, declining gradually across the number of semesters enrolled. The probability of graduation from WCC coincides with the probability of four-year transfer after seven semesters at WCC, thereafter remaining substantially above the probability of four-year transfer. Similarly, the probability of WCC graduation coincides with the probability of stopout at eight semesters, thereafter exceeding the latter.

Overall, the survival analysis shows a wide range of enrollment and outcome behavior reflecting great complexity among community college students of this institution. For example, for the most part, transfer to a four-year institution is about equally probable for up to seven semesters enrolled at WCC. A similar statement can be made about transfer to a two-year institution. On the other hand, earning a degree or certificate increases in probability over that same number of semesters.

For this cohort at least, amidst the complexity there appear to be three roughly discernable stages of enrollment and outcome activity. Despite their fuzziness at the boundaries, the stages can be used as a rough lens through which to observe the eclectic behavior of community college students. The first stage covers enrollment from one to four semesters. Overall, this is a highly *dynamic* period. The probability of stopout is at its highest after the first semester, transfer to a four-year institution reaches its highest probability after the second semester at WCC, and the probability of both events decreases after the third semester. An outcome of transfer to another two-year institution is less probable during this period. After the fourth semester, there is a jump in probability of attainment of a WCC degree or certificate.

The second stage occurs between five and seven semesters. This stage is marked by a leveling off of probability for both transfer to a four-year institution and stopout. Degree attainment jumps before it also levels off at six and seven semesters. The third stage emerges after seven semesters of enrollment. This stage could be labeled decisive for every outcome, since after this point the general direction of the probability of each outcome is established for the remainder of the period, with the singular exception of graduation, where the highest values are reached after the ninth semester and followed by a distinct (downward) change in probability. In subsequent research (not reflected in results presented here), the pattern of the three stages labeled dynamic, level, and decisive generally held for students who first enrolled at WCC in Fall 2000 and Fall 2002 as well. Clearly, the four outcomes are extended in time, with noticeable numbers of each outcome throughout all terms. This suggests that the utilization of the community college to realize outcomes over time is highly diffuse.

Independent Variables: Descriptive Analysis

We next investigated the effects of a number of independent variables on outcome. The independent variables in our study included gender, ethnicity, educational attainment prior to WCC, first-semester education goal, and cumulative GPA. Age is shown in Table 3, but was excluded from the inferential analysis in Table 4 because it is a time-dependent variable and beyond the scope of this

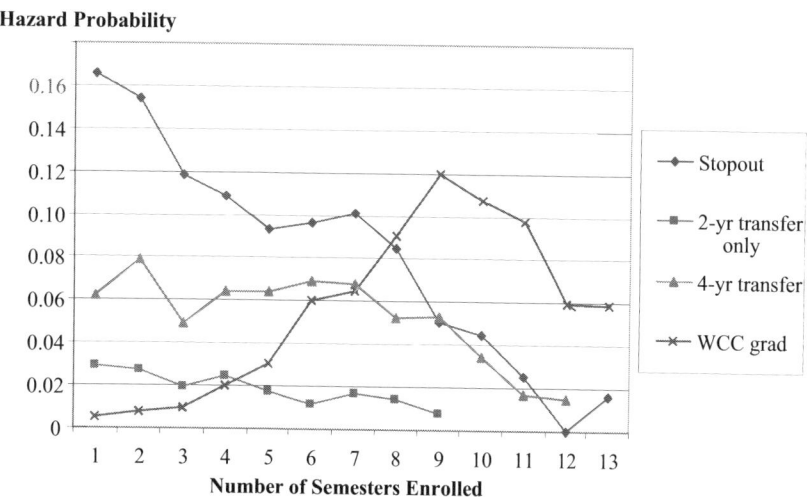

Figure 1. Probability of Outcome by Number of Semesters Enrolled

study. All variables were categorized due to the nature of the statistical analysis.

In the frequency distribution displayed in Table 3, the largest demographic groups for all outcomes except stopout were female, in the 17-19 age group, and Caucasian students. For the stopout category, the proportion of males was about the same as females and the 25-50 age group (36%) comprised about the same proportion as the 17-19 age group (35%). For the cumulative GPA variable, a total of about 50% of students who fell in the outcome categories of stopout or two-year transfer had cumulative GPAs in the 2.00-3.99 range. For the other outcomes, four-year transfer and WCC graduate, the same range of cumulative GPA prevailed (72% and 81% respectively). This distribution suggests that the latter outcomes are more likely to happen with the higher GPA students.

The educational attainment categories prior to enrollment at WCC included no prior college enrollment, prior two-year college experience, and prior four-year college experience. The no prior college enrollment category, which constitutes 60% of the cohort, represented the largest proportions across all outcomes. The first-semester educational goal categories were associate's degrees with or without transfer, certificates with or without transfer, transfer only, and job/personal interest/other. The goal of associate's degree attainment, with or without transfer, had the largest proportions in all outcomes except four-year transfer. In this last outcome category, the largest proportion was transfer-only goal (43%), followed closely by associate's degrees with or without transfer at 41%.

Main Effects of Independent Variables

Cox regression analysis was used to analyze the factors that contribute to the occurrence of an event known as risk factors (Cox and Oakes, 1984). Since each student can attain one of four outcomes (or "events" in survival analysis terminology), which are mutually exclusive and exhaustive, each outcome can be said to "compete" with the others for occurrence. Current enrollees (students enrolled at WCC in the 13th or last term), who have not yet experienced any outcome, are censored. In addition, each outcome is modeled such that the other three outcomes are treated as censored. For example, when modeling stopout, all other outcomes are considered as censored observations. This allows investigation of the effects of independent variables on risk of stopout to differ from those associated with other outcomes such as risk of transfer

Table 3. Distribution of Outcome by Selected Variables

	Current Enrollee* (N = 173)		Stopout (N = 1,593)		2-Year Transfer (N = 276)		4-Year Transfer (N = 801)		WCC Graduate (N = 376)	
	n	%	n	%	n	%	n	%	n	%
Gender										
Female	98	57%	785	49%	162	59%	420	53%	248	66%
Male	75	43%	808	51%	114	41%	379	47%	127	34%
Age in Fall 2001										
<17	3	2%	19	1%	1	0%	28	3%	13	3%
17-19	97	56%	560	35%	145	53%	390	49%	180	48%
20-24	29	17%	328	21%	74	27%	217	27%	67	18%
25-50	38	22%	577	36%	54	20%	141	18%	107	28%
>50	4	2%	65	4%	1	0%	5	1%	3	1%
Ethnicity										
Asian	1	1%	117	7%	13	5%	59	7%	27	7%
African-American	22	13%	224	14%	38	14%	86	11%	42	11%
Caucasian	131	76%	1025	64%	193	70%	539	67%	247	66%
All other	11	6%	117	7%	21	8%	51	6%	38	10%
Prior Education Level										
No college enrollment	121	70%	981	62%	177	64%	401	50%	257	68%
2-year graduate/transfer from community college	24	14%	174	11%	50	18%	58	7%	47	13%
4-year graduate/transfer from 4-year college	28	16%	438	27%	49	18%	342	43%	72	19%
1st Semester Education Goal										
Associate's degree with or without transfer	125	72%	750	47%	156	57%	329	41%	274	73%
Certificate with or without transfer	22	13%	223	14%	28	10%	34	4%	73	19%
Transfer only	14	8%	267	17%	55	20%	342	43%	16	4%
Job/personal interest/other	12	7%	341	21%	35	13%	94	12%	10	3%
Cumulative GPA										
GPA=0	3	2%	101	6%	22	8%	23	3%	0	0%
.01<=GPA<=1.99	8	5%	259	16%	51	18%	48	6%	2	1%
2.0<=GPA<=2.99	74	43%	344	22%	76	28%	212	26%	83	22%
3.0<=GPA<=3.99	80	46%	447	28%	64	23%	371	46%	261	69%
GPA=4.0	6	3%	202	13%	23	8%	97	12%	30	8%
No GPA	2	1%	240	15%	40	14%	50	6%	0	0%

*Censored cases

Note: Percentages within a category may not sum to 100; observations based on unknown/no response are included in calculations but do not appear in table.

or graduation. In other words, the same variable can have a different effect depending on the outcome being modeled.

Table 4 indicates the analysis of a given variable on all four types of outcome compared to other categories within the variable. The cell values are hazard ratios, which can be interpreted like odds ratios in logistic regression. Unlike the latter, however, they cannot be considered predictive since the timing of event or outcome occurrence is what is being investigated (Chen, 2005). Like an odds ratio, for each variable the hazard ratio represents likelihood relative to a referent category, which is indicated in parentheses in Table 4.

The variables of statistical significance are demographics, followed by educational background, goal, and academic performance (based on cumulative GPA at WCC). Female students were about 37% more likely to transfer to a two-year college than male students and 92% as likely as the males to transfer to a four-year institution. Ethnicity was associated with outcome only for Asian students, who were 50% more likely to graduate at WCC than Caucasian students.

Students who were enrolled at another postsecondary institution prior to WCC (transfer or prior degree), were significantly more likely to stopout and twice as likely to transfer (to a two- or four-year college) than students with no college prior to WCC. First-semester educational goal was significantly associated with each outcome except transfer to a two-year college. As one would expect, students with a non-academic goal (job, personal interest) were more than twice as likely to stopout, compared to students who sought to earn a WCC associate's degree (with or without transfer) and half as likely to graduate from WCC. However, the former were also 40% more likely to transfer than the associate's degree, with or without transfer group. Not surprisingly, students with a goal of transfer without earning a WCC degree or certificate were four times more likely to transfer to a four-year college and half as likely to graduate from WCC as the associate's degree with or without transfer group.

Most prominently, cumulative GPA at WCC was associated with outcome. The calculation here used the $3.0 \leq GPA \leq 3.99$ group as the referent group, because it had a larger number of students than each of the other GPA categories. The finding that GPA was highly significant is consistent with and extends previous work that found graduation was predicted by GPA (Ronco, 1996). The $3.0 \leq GPA \leq 3.99$ group was much less likely to stopout or transfer to a two-year college than the other GPA groups and more likely to graduate from WCC or transfer to a four-year college than lower GPA groups. The GPA = 4.0 group was more likely to transfer to a two-year or four-year college and more than twice as likely to graduate at WCC than the $3.0 \leq GPA \leq 3.99$ group. In general, students with a GPA below 3.0 were more likely to stopout or transfer to a two-year college, while those with a GPA above 3.0 were more likely to graduate or transfer to a four-year college.

Interaction Effects of Time

The analysis of the main effects of independent variables using Cox regression analysis assumes that each variable has an identical effect in each time period (semester). This assumption that the hazard functions for two different levels of a covariate are proportional for all values of the time variable is known as the assumption of proportional hazards (Ronco, 1996). However, as explained by Ronco (1996), it is quite possible that there can be interaction effects between covariates and time, such that the former can have a different impact on hazard at different points in time. The interaction effect is tested mathematically by forming cross products in the data set between the time and the independent variable and then including those cross products, along with the relevant main effects, as variables in the hazard model (Singer & Willett, 1993; Ronco, 1996).

One way to test whether this assumption is met is to construct and examine a log-minus-log (LML) plot of the survival function, which is the same as the log transformation of hazard function. If the proportional hazards assumption is met, the lines generated by LML should be parallel and separated by a roughly constant vertical difference. In this study, for example, if males have twice the risk of stopout compared to females after first semester enrolled and the proportional hazards assumption holds, males should also have twice the risk of stopout as females after any semester enrolled.

Figures 2a through 2f depict the LML plot for selected independent variables. Each line represents the log transformation of hazard function at mean of covariates. If there is no interaction between the independent variable and time, these lines are separated by a roughly constant vertical difference (as in Figure 2a, the bottom two lines in Figure 2b, and the first two lines in Figure 2e). If the lines are not roughly parallel and cross each other, there is interaction between the independent variable and time, and the analysis of main effects above would not hold across all time periods.

More specifically, Figure 2b implies that the upper line is the log transformation of hazard function for students whose highest educational level prior to WCC was at least college coursework in a two-year college and no higher prior attainment than a two-year degree. The middle and bottom lines represent the log transformation of hazard functions for students with no college experience, and for students who had coursework or degrees from four-year institutions, respectively. The fact that the line for two-year coursework/graduate is higher than the others reflects that the former is at greater risk of transfer to a two-year college than the latter. While the two bottom lines are separated by a roughly constant vertical difference across terms as mentioned above, the vertical difference of the first two lines decreases as the total terms increase. This means that there is interaction effect of time between students who had two-year coursework/graduate and students with no college experience on the outcome of two-year transfer. Where the distance between lines changes noticeably (the first two lines in Figures 2b, 2c, and 2f) and particularly if lines intersect (as in the two bottom lines in Figure 2c), the graphs suggest the presence of an interaction effect of time with the independent variables. Although some of the lines in Figure 2d seem to have interaction effects of time, this may be disregarded since cross products in the data set between the time and the independent variable were not statistically significant (based on results in Table 5).

Table 5 summarizes the effects of independent variables on different events after accounting for interaction effects of time. A (+) indicates a variable group is likely to have a shorter time to the corresponding outcome than the compared referent group (shown in parentheses for each variable); (-) indicates a group is less likely to have a shorter time to event. The presence of an asterisk next to (+) or (-) indicates that the variable had differential effects on an outcome category involving time that were significant. For example, after taking interaction with time into account, female students were significantly more likely to graduate from WCC than male students.

Before taking time into account, there was not a statistically significant difference for graduation (as shown in Table 4). Another instance of the significant effect of time involved the likelihood of transfer to a four-year college by students who had prior educational experience at the two-year college level, compared with students who did not have any college experience before WCC.

A (+) or (-) without an asterisk in Table 5 means that there was a significant differential effect with no accompanying interaction effect involving time. This situation, no interaction effect with time, is most noticeable for the effect of GPA on stopout and on graduation from WCC and for the effect of educational goal on stopout. In contrast, the significant effect of GPA on the two-year transfer outcome that existed before considering time was still present with a significant time interaction.

The "0" indicates that the parameter estimates were not statistically significant for the outcome after taking time interaction into account. In some cases, the effect of time resulted in a change from a statistically significant to a non-significant relationship. Examples of this result were the effect of being Asian on graduation from WCC, and the effect of the job/personal interest goal on transfer to a four-year college and on graduation from WCC. However, while Table 5 shows that there were a few changes on the main effects due to interaction with time, one can conclude that overall this was not a significant factor. Thus, the assumption of proportional hazards is justified, and the interpretation of main effects based on results in Table 4 is reasonable.

Table 4. Estimated Effects of Selected Variables on the Probability of Realizing Outcome

Variables	Stopout	2-Year Transfer	4-Year Transfer	WCC Graduate
Gender				
Female (vs. male)	0.900*	1.367*	0.920	1.233
Ethnicity				
Asian (vs. Caucasian)	0.937	0.600	1.020	1.571*
African-American (vs. Caucasian)	1.042	0.801	1.100	1.201
All other (vs. Caucasian)	0.932	0.792	0.846	1.206
Prior Education Level				
2-year graduate/transfer from community college (vs. no college enrollment)	1.224*	1.987***	1.013	1.022
4-year graduate/transfer from 4-year college (vs. no college enrollment)	1.159*	0.829	2.198***	1.034
1st Semester Education Goal				
Certificate with or without transfer (vs. associate's degree with or without transfer)	1.491***	1.006	0.518***	1.755***
Transfer only (vs. associate's degree with or without transfer)	1.170*	1.221	3.952***	0.497**
Job/personal interest/other (vs. associate's with or without transfer)	2.341***	1.382	1.420**	0.481*
Cumulative GPA				
GPA=0 (vs. $3.0 \leq GPA \leq 3.99$)	5.862***	8.853***	1.453	0.000
$.01 \leq GPA \leq 1.99$ (vs. $3.0 \leq GPA \leq 3.99$)	3.057***	4.224***	0.574***	0.083***
$2.0 \leq GPA \leq 2.99$ (vs. $3.0 \leq GPA \leq 3.99$)	1.229**	1.937***	0.863	0.494***
GPA=4.0 (vs. $3.0 \leq GPA \leq 3.99$)	2.744***	2.659***	1.724***	2.277***
No GPA (vs. $3.0 \leq GPA \leq 3.99$)	6.387***	8.737***	2.133***	0.000

Effects are expressed as exponential of the estimated parameters. A hazard rate ratio of 1.00 means that the variable has no effect on the probability of outcome. *p<.05   **p<.01   ***p<.001

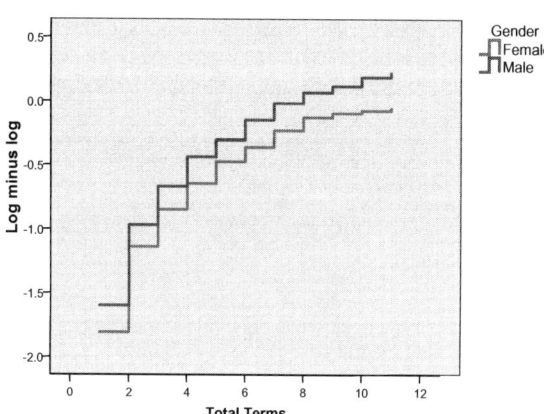

Figure 2a. LML Plot of Gender on Risk of Stopout

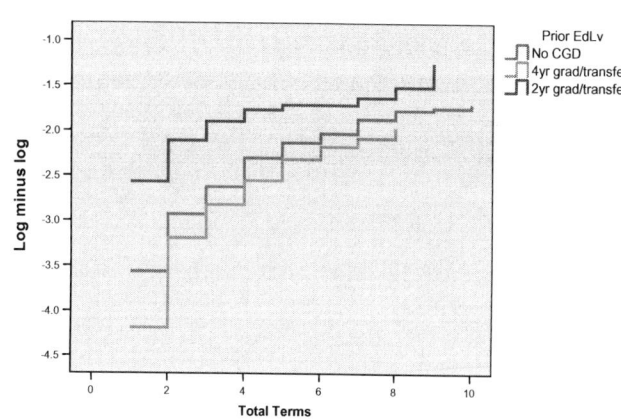

Figure 2b. LML plot of Prior Education Level on Risk of 2-Year Transfer

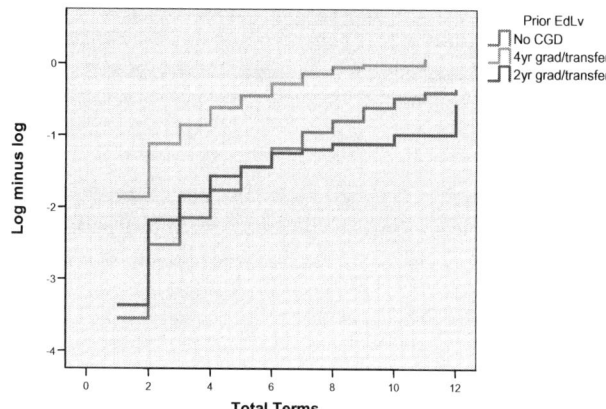

Figure 2c. LML Plot of Prior Education Level on Risk of 4-Year Transfer

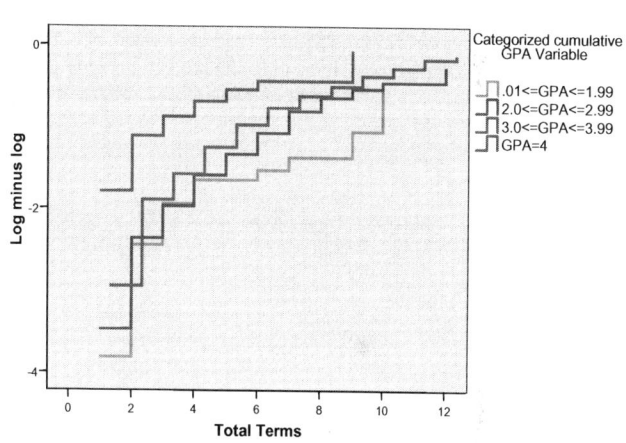

Figure 2d. LML Plot of Cumulated GPA on Risk of 4-Year Transfer

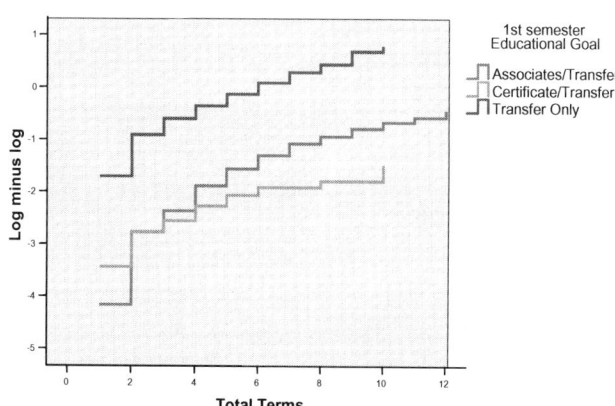

Figure 2e. LML Plot of 1st Semester Education Goal on Risk of 4-Year Transfer

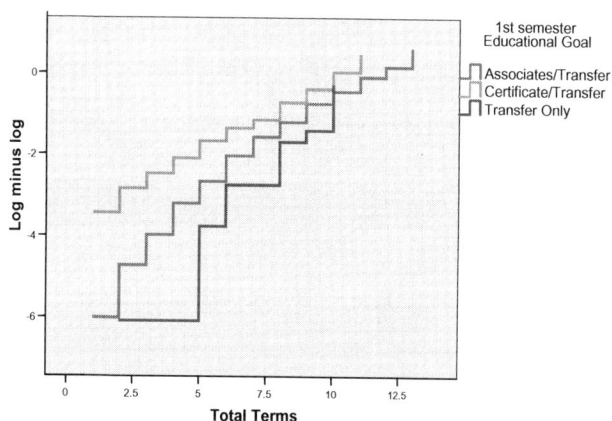

Figure 2f. LML plot of 1st Semester Education Goal on Risk of Graduation

Conclusion

The purposes of this study were to explore the complexity of student enrollment behavior in a community college cohort and to analyze outcome attainment by using a competing risks survival analysis model. During the 13 semesters of the study period, the largest number of academic outcomes was transfer to a four-year university or college, which is the most popular goal of community college students. Less than half that number of students, 12% of the total cohort, graduated from this institution during the period under study.

With a wide range of enrollment patterns and outcome behavior within the study period, there appear to be three roughly discernable stages labeled as dynamic, leveling off, and decisive. Stopout rate peaks after the first semester and remains high relative to the other outcomes up to seven semesters. Transfer to a four-year institution peaks after the second semester and it remains high relative to the two outcomes, two-year transfer and graduation, until the same number of semesters. Although the graduation rate peaks after nine semesters, it remains high relative to the other outcomes to the endpoint of this study.

Examining the correlates of each outcome category confirmed much of what could be reasonably expected. The GPA variable can be an important factor for understanding student enrollment behavior. Students who have an academic goal and perform well in college courses are more likely to graduate or transfer to a four-year college. Students who had two-year college experience were more likely to transfer to either a two- or four-year college, while students with four-year college experience were more likely to transfer to a four-year college than students with no college experience.

However, this study is not conclusive because of issues that arise in assessing the validity of the model assumptions. It is difficult to make judgments about the proportional hazards on the LML plot of survival curves, partly because the functions are non-linear instead of straight lines (Chen, 2005). This limitation may be resolved with the smoothed plots of the scaled Schoenfeld residuals proposed by Therneau and Grambsch (van Belle, Fisher, Heagerty, & Lumley, 2004). Another limitation of this study is that it treats all stopouts alike regardless of enrollment frequency. The research could be extended to develop a definition of dropout based on an empirical analysis of the length of the period of no enrollment through the last semester under study. Moreover, the effects of the independent variables that change during time, such as age, were not included in this study since the hazard ratios change over time. To include time-dependent variables in the analysis, the extended Cox regression method could be used (Chen, 2005).

Using the competing risks survival analysis model helps us to understand the timing of enrollment behavior associated with the four basic outcomes of community colleges cov-

Table 5. Summary of Differential Effects of Variables on Outcome Over Time

Variables	Stopout	2-Year Transfer	4-Year Transfer	WCC Graduate
Gender				
Female (vs. male)	0	(+)	0	(+)*
Ethnicity				
Asian (vs. Caucasian)	0	0	0	0
African-American (vs. Caucasian)	0	0	0	0
All other (vs. Caucasian)	0	0	0	0
Prior Education Level				
2-year graduate/transfer from community college (vs. no college enrollment)	(+)	(+)*	(+)*	0
4-year graduate/transfer from 4-year college (vs. no college enrollment)	(+)	0	(+)*	0
1st Semester Education Goal				
Certificate with or without transfer (vs. associate's degree with or without transfer)	(+)	0	(−)	(+)*
Transfer only (vs. associate's degree with or without transfer)	(+)	0	(+)	0
Job/personal interest/other (vs. associate's degree with or without transfer)	(+)	0	0	0
Categorized Cumulative GPA				
GPA=0 (vs. 3.0 ≤GPA≤3.99)	(+)	(+)*	0	0
.01≤GPA≤1.99 (vs. 3.0≤GPA≤3.99)	(+)	(+)*	(−)	(−)
2.0≤GPA≤2.99 (vs. 3.0≤GPA≤3.99)	(+)	(+)*	0	(−)
GPA=4.0 (vs. 3.0≤GPA≤3.99)	(+)	(+)*	0	(+)
No GPA (vs. 3.0≤GPA≤3.99)	(+)	(+)*	0	0

Note: (−) Parameter estimates negative, p < .05
(+) Parameter estimates positive, p < .05
0 Parameter estimates are not significant
*Interaction with time variable, p < .05

ered in this study and the role that various factors contribute toward the attainment of these outcomes. Over one-quarter of the total cohort stopped out after one or two semesters enrolled in this institution. For this reason, it would be beneficial to observe in a future study what other factors may be associated with stopout students. The model could also be applied to further investigations that would include variables in addition to those covered in this study, such as major, financial aid, and enrollment status.

References

Adelman, C. (2005). *Moving into town – and moving on: The community college in the lives of traditional-age students*. Washington, DC: U.S. Department of Education.

Chen, C.K. (2005). *Analyzing student learning outcomes: Usefulness of logistic and Cox regression models*. IR Applications, 5, 1-18.

Cox, D.R., & Oaks, D. (1984). *Analysis of survival data*. London: Chapman and Hall.

DesJardins, S. L. (2003). *Event history methods: Conceptual issues and an application to student departure from college*. Higher Education: Handbook of Theory and Research, XVIII, 421-472.

Porter, S. R. (2002). *Including transfer-out behavior in retention models: Using the NSC enrollment search data* (AIR Professional File No. 82). Tallahassee, FL: Association for Institutional Research.

Ronco, S. L. (1996). *How enrollment ends: Analyzing the correlates of student graduation, transfer and dropout with a competing risks model* (AIR Professional File No. 61). Tallahassee, FL: Association for Institutional Research.

Singer, J. D., & Willett, J. B. (1991). *Modeling the days of our lives: Using survival analysis when designing longitudinal studies of duration and timing of events*. Psychological Bulletin, 110, 268-290.

Singer, J. D., & Willett, J. B. (1993). It's about time: Using discrete-time survival analysis to study duration and the timing of events. *Journal of Educational Statistics, 18*, 155-195.

van Belle, G. T., Fisher, L. D., Heagerty, P. J., & Lumley, T. (2004). *Biostatistics: A Methodology for the Health Sciences* (2nd Edition). Wiley InterScience.

Voorhees, R.A., Smith, G. P., & Luan, J. (2006). Researching student transitions. *Journal of Applied Research in the Community College, 13*(2), 177-188.

Dr. Roger Mourad, *PhD, JD is Director of the Institutional Research Department at Washtenaw Community College in Ann Arbor, Michigan. He can be contacted at mou@wccnet.org.*

Ji-Hee Hong, *MS, is a Research Analyst at Washtenaw Community College in Ann Arbor, Michigan. She can be contacted at jhong@wccnet.org.*

Who Are Our Students? Cluster Analysis as a Tool for Understanding Community College Student Populations

Bridget V. Ammon
University of Michigan

Jamillah Bowman
Stanford University

Roger Mourad
Washtenaw Community College

This study showcases cluster analysis as a useful tool for those who seek to understand the types of students their community colleges serve. Although educational goal, academic program, and demographics are often used as descriptive variables, it is unclear which, if any, of these are the best way to classify community college students. Cluster analyses at two points in time each identified nine distinct clusters in our data. These clusters had a 67% overlap, indicating method validity and consistency over time. The differences between the two years could be due to differences in enrollment over time, but are likely a result of changes in questions asked of the students from year one to year two. The results of this study suggest the utility of cluster analysis as a way for stakeholders to describe and classify their students. Furthermore, once established, cluster membership can be used to predict later success, usage of student services, and other important outcomes. When administrators understand these differences among students, they can better serve all groups of students and identify ways to market to them and address their unique needs.

Introduction

As with other postsecondary institutions, comprehensive community colleges must develop systematic ways to better understand and serve an increasingly diversified student population. Washtenaw Community College (WCC) serves such a student body, with students coming from various backgrounds and pursuing a wide range of academic goals. A better understanding of this complex student body can help inform program planning, policy, and student services initiatives. For a college to effectively develop and market services to students, it is essential to have a portrait of the student body.

The following two studies utilized cluster analysis to create a profile of our community college students that will ultimately help us better understand the students we serve. The first study was primarily descriptive to lay the foundation for future research; replication in the second study served as a method validation tool. In future studies, we will do more in-depth analyses to investigate which of the "clusters" of students identified are most likely to succeed and how effective student services are at reaching different clusters. This information could be used to help college decision makers identify issues that affect student success, effectively address them through appropriate student services initiatives, and better define the target audiences for services and marketing.

Traditionally, community colleges as a whole serve students of different ages, socioeconomic statuses, and backgrounds (Schuetz, 2002). Several important trends are apparent in the present literature concerning community college enrollment. First, it is clear that students enroll in community colleges for a variety of reasons, including personal enrichment, career goals, and intent to transfer (Bryant, 2001). Some students intend to earn a degree at the community college level, while others are non-credit or transfer students. Over time, the ethnic diversity of community college populations has increased (Bryant, 2001), and there are increasing numbers of students who would benefit from remediation (Schuetz, 2002). Community colleges are serving more dually-enrolled high school students and reverse transfer students who have received college degrees from other institutions (Andrews, 2003). The product of these trends is a more diverse community college student body, which needs a wide variety of support and services.

It is crucial for community college educators, administrators, and other stakeholders to understand the student bodies of their colleges. Such an exploration provides stakeholders with an idea of the types of services that are necessary, for whom, and how to design and market them effectively. Previous research has sometimes chosen to focus on one dimension of the student body, and to describe profiles of types of students based on that characteristic. For example, VanDerLinden (2002) categorized a national sample of community college students according to their primary reason for enrollment. Based on these profiles, she described differences in areas such as academic field, racial background, and age. She also used the "reason for enrollment" categorization to predict satisfaction with academic advising, career change, and academic growth and competence.

Although it can be useful to choose a variable by which to categorize students based on theoretical or practical questions, these categorizations may be arbitrary or misleading. In order to allow the data to better inform decisions concerning the variables that are the most distinguishing factors for a given sample, cluster analysis can be used. Of course, the researcher determines the variables to enter into the analysis; however, the statistical results permit the researcher to explore the possibility that some variables are more influential than others in characterizing a sample. In one study, this statistical method was used to cluster community colleges, and it was found that size and sector were the two most distinguishing features in creating clusters of institutions (Phipps, Shedd, Merisotis, & Carroll, 2001).

Cluster analysis was also used to create a profile of students in another community college, similar to our purposes in this study. In a sample from Prince George's Community College, Boughan (2000) described how achievement-related variables formed interesting and meaningful clusters. This typology allowed the researcher to examine clusters that may have been more at-risk and how to appropriately target those students to increase retention.

In the present study, we used cluster analyses to form a profile of the WCC student body. We explored three different types of student variables: background characteristics, academic pursuits, and reason for enrolling. The population of students enrolling in community colleges is not static, and in fact changes frequently over time (Bryant, 2001). WCC serves traditional and non-traditional aged college students who come from different cultures and ethnicities. There are significant numbers of students that have previous higher education experience at other institutions when they enroll at WCC. Our goal was to discern whether students can be clustered into discrete categories on the basis of these demographic characteristics, academic variables, or intent variables.

Certain critical choices are made by community college students before and during their enrollment that determine how they approach and interact with the academic institution and the academic process. These choices include what subjects students study, how heavily they will engage in the college experience, and what types of degrees they seek. As a community college, WCC offers a wide range of options to students with a variety of needs and goals. These options include liberal arts transfer programs, occupational programs, vocational or technical programs, non-credit programs, and college preparation classes. Students can elect to study full-time or part-time and they can choose from a range of academic majors. Some enroll to earn a degree and some to acquire extra skills or credits. Some students are simultaneously enrolled at WCC and a local high school or four-year institution and many students work full-time. Analyzing our students' academic choices simultaneously with their backgrounds and reasons for enrolling will help us better understand the "types" of students who commonly make certain academic choices.

Prior research suggested that educational goal is a variable that forms heterogeneous groups of students (VanDerLinden, 2002). Those enrolling for work-related goals are often the non-traditional, older, fully-employed part-time students. Furthermore, students with an intention to transfer tend to be younger and more likely to enroll full-time. Another variable that has been useful in clustering students is academic achievement (Boughan, 2000). The following cluster analysis was intended to provide us with a preliminary indication of whether these patterns are present at WCC, or if any other interesting profiles emerge for WCC students. As cluster analysis is a descriptive method rather than an inferential method, we did not enter into the study with specific hypotheses, but used our knowledge of our student body, and community colleges in general, to guide the statistical choices we had to make.

Study 1: Method Establishment

Sample

This analysis was based upon data obtained from the Current Student Survey (CSS), which is administered by the institutional research staff at WCC each fall semester. With an average student headcount of 12,000 each fall, the survey provides college administrators, professional staff, and faculty with useful information about WCC students and how they intend to use their education. The sample for this particular study was the respondents of the 2001 survey, a random sample of 403 students. In addition to survey data, this study incorporated student data from the WCC institutional information system.

The sample included degree and non-degree students from a wide variety of backgrounds and academic interests. About 50% of the survey respondents were female and 18% were students of color (African American, Hispanic, Asian, Native American, or Other). Nearly half of the sample had previous higher education experience, almost half (48%) were employed full time, and 27% were enrolled full time. Other than an over-representation of new students, the sample was comparable to the total student body at WCC in Fall 2001. See Table 1 for more detailed descriptive sample data on key variables.

Measures

The variables of interest in this cluster analysis can be categorized into three major groups–demographic, academic, and educational goals. There were theoretical and practical reasons for these choices. Theoretically, demographic variables were included to determine how diversity in terms of race, ethnicity, gender, and age might be critical for understanding students (Bryant, 2001). Academic variables were included because previous research at the community college level suggested the importance of academic status (Boughan, 2000). Educational goal has also been identified as a critical variable for grouping students (VanDerLinden, 2002). Practically speaking, all of our variables were also chosen because they are traditionally available to community college administrators and institutional researchers; therefore, our study methodology should be easily transferred to other settings.

Prior to cluster analysis, we transformed all categorical and continuous variables into dichotomous variables. This process simplified the final analysis by giving the data a substantive meaning as percentages of students who had a certain characteristic and provided a means of standardizing our variables.

Demographic Variables: The first group of variables included in the analysis was a set of demographic variables that provided an idea of what backgrounds and life circumstances the students brought to WCC. Demographic variables of interest were: minority status (African-American, Hispanic, Asian, Native American, and Other), female, older student (age 25+), previous higher education (college graduates or transfers from other two-year or four-year institutions), in-district (Washtenaw County), and employed full-time (30 hours or more per week).

Academic Variables: The second group consisted of academic-related variables that captured the students' academic status and interests at WCC. These included: high GPA (>3.5 at end of Fall 2001), new student, study load (full-time/part-time), dual enrollment (currently enrolled at another institution — high school or college), non-degree (referring to students who did not enroll in a degree program), spoke frequently with faculty outside of class (3 or more times a semester being coded as high), and academic program. The five academic programs referred to in this paper are: Business and Computer Technology (BCT), Health and Applied Technology (HAT), Humanities and Social Sciences (HSS), Mathematics, Natural and Behavioral Sciences (MNB), and Technology non-degree.

Educational Goal: The final group of variables captured the students' intended use of their WCC education. This was a question asked on the CSS during Fall 2001. The variables included: work-related reasons (pay raise/promotion, new job, learn new skills for work, etc.), to transfer credits, and for personal satisfaction (accomplishment, status, enjoyment/hobbyist, etc.). There was also a separate variable asking whether the student planned to transfer his or her credits, because approximately 18% of the students that primarily enroll for work or personal reasons also plan on transferring WCC credits to a four-year college or university.

Analytic Method: Cluster Analysis

Cluster analysis is a multivariate procedure for detecting groupings in data that sorts cases into clusters that "are maximally within-group homogeneous and without-group heterogeneous" (Boughan, 2000; p. 11). In other words, the method provides the researcher with clusters that are as different from each other as possible, with the members within each cluster as similar to each other as possible. With this method, a researcher can use knowledge from previous research or practical experience with the student body to guide decisions such as the number of clusters that may emerge and which variables might distinguish those clusters. However, it is an iterative process and each consecutive solution informs the next iteration of the analysis. Cluster analysis is a good empirical technique to use in exploratory data analysis when the sample is suspected to be heterogeneous in important ways.

With cluster analysis, variables with large values contribute more to the calculations than those with small values. Therefore, before starting the analysis, the variables should be standardized by transforming each into a z-score or by dummy coding the variables. In this case, we dummy coded the variables of interest using binary "0" or "1" coding (for absent and present, respectively). We used pairwise deletion of missing data in order to lose the minimal amount of data.

There are two major clustering methods: hierarchical cluster analysis and k-means cluster analysis (Aldenderfer & Blashfield, 1984). Both methods have useful features that should be considered before conducting a cluster analysis. In this study, we used k-means, which can easily handle large sample sizes. Once the data are prepared for the analysis, the researcher has to specify the number of clusters and then the mathematically optimum

Table 1. Descriptive Statistics of Survey Respondents (2001) Compared to Overall WCC Student Body

Characteristic	Sample % (*n* = 403)	Overall WCC % (*N* = 11,171)
Minority	18	28
Female	51	55
Over 25	49	52
In District	69	69
Previous Higher Education	48	44
New-Student Status	53	29
Full-Time Enrollment	27	25
Non-Degree	45	39

case sort for that number of clusters is calculated. The k-means procedure starts by using the values of the first k cases as temporary estimates of the cluster means; initial cluster centers are formed by assigning each case to the cluster with the most similar cluster center, then updating the center. Lastly, an iterative process determines the final cluster centers. For the purposes of this report, we were uncertain of the sufficient number of clusters that would provide us with a comprehensive yet parsimonious set of profiles; therefore, we looked at a range of solutions from 5-15 clusters.

The *F* statistic in k-means one-way Analysis of Variance (ANOVA) is calculated to help identify variables that drive the clustering, as well as those that vary little across clusters. A large *F* value means that the variable was an important factor in the analysis. The researcher should note the *size* of the *F* statistic only; the significance level does not provide useful information since the clusters are formed to be as different from one another as possible and are thus almost by definition statistically significant (Aldenderfer & Blashfield, 1984). It is also important to check the number of cases in each cluster, because cases are not necessarily equally distributed across clusters. However, fewer cases do not necessarily invalidate the meaningfulness of a cluster; it simply indicates that there are fewer students characterized by that type.

The next step is to examine descriptive statistics on key variables for each cluster and compare the differences between groups. In order to do this, one must save the cluster membership for each case and tabulate these values against other categorical variables of interest. Finally, the researcher thoroughly examines each cluster to interpret what "type" of student it characterizes based on the personality of the cluster and conceptualizes a meaningful name for each cluster based on these findings. In our final analysis, all clusters could be named and each seemed to produce a meaningful category of students. This section is provided as only an introduction to cluster analysis; for further information, researchers should begin with Aldenderfer and Blashfield (1984).

Results for Study 1

After combining the results of several cluster analyses with our own theoretical and practical knowledge concerning the types of students that attend WCC, our final cluster solution identified nine different student sub-bodies, each providing useful information about common patterns within a diverse student population. As indicated by the high *F* values, the cluster formation was primarily driven by the student's educational goal and whether he/she enrolled as a non-degree student or pursued a certificate or an associate's degree (See Table 2 for *F* statistics). Variables such as GPA, gender, race, residency, new-student status, and full-time enrollment had lower *F* values, suggesting that they played less of a role in differentiating clusters.

Further analysis of the specific characteristics identifying each of the nine clusters revealed three primary categories described below: *Skill Upgraders, Career Advancers,* and *Transfer Students* (See Figure 1). These three categories reflect students' reasons for enrolling and were created post-hoc as a framework to better organize the presentation of these nine clusters, which were statistically determined by our analyses using k-means cluster analysis in SPSS ver. 13.0.

Skill Upgrader Clusters

In general, Skill Upgraders were those students who enrolled in WCC to increase their skills and knowledge for personal reasons.

Table 2. One-Way Analysis of Variance Results for Nine-Cluster Solution

Demographics	Between Cluster Mean Square	Within Cluster Mean Square	F
Minority	0.791	0.136	5.818
Female	0.971	0.236	4.117
Over 25	4.589	0.161	28.52
In District	1.079	0.196	5.504
Previous Higher Ed	1.942	0.216	9.007
Employed Full-Time	1.603	0.223	7.202
Academic			
New-Student Status	0.833	0.238	3.496
>3.5 GPA	0.449	0.246	1.824
Dual Enrollment	1.777	0.037	48.405
Full-Time Enrollment	0.228	0.196	1.163
Non-Degree	10.941	0.029	375.588
Associate's Degree	10.359	0.032	326.073
Certificate	4.085	0.045	91.019
BCT	4.453	0.135	33.021
HAT	1.724	0.115	14.975
MNB	0.231	0.116	1.997
HSS	1.552	0.166	9.378
Tech, Unspecified	0.465	0.076	6.132
Talk to Faculty	0.539	0.236	2.281
Primary Reason For Enrolling			
Work	10.114	0.045	225.361
Transfer	10.557	0.03	349.632
Personal	4.69	0.041	113.149
Transfer to 4 Year	6.837	0.117	58.665

Students characterized as Skill Upgraders made up 16% of the total sample. This category consisted of two clusters: the Personal Enrichment cluster and the Non-Traditional Student cluster. These students were almost all non-degree or certificate students. Overall, the Skill Upgraders were those with previous higher education experience and who enrolled for personal reasons (See Table 3). Furthermore, the Skill Upgraders tended to be in-district students over the age of 25.

Cluster 1: Personal Enrichment (9.9%). About half of the Personal Enrichment students were employed full-time, but they did not take classes for work-related purposes. Almost all students in this cluster lived in-district. These tended to be non-degree students who were taking classes for their own enrichment in the culinary arts, graphic arts, and business.

Cluster 2: Non-Traditional Students (6.2%). This cluster was named non-traditional students because of an overrepresentation of traditionally underrepresented groups, as well as the fact that most students traveled from other districts to attend WCC. Unlike the Personal Enrichment students, most of the Non-Traditional Students came from outside of Washtenaw County and a majority of them were female and minority students (80% and 67%, respectively). In fact, this cluster had the largest proportion of minority students across all clusters ($p < .05$). In terms of academic characteristics, many of the Non-Traditional Students were new to WCC, were pursuing certificates,

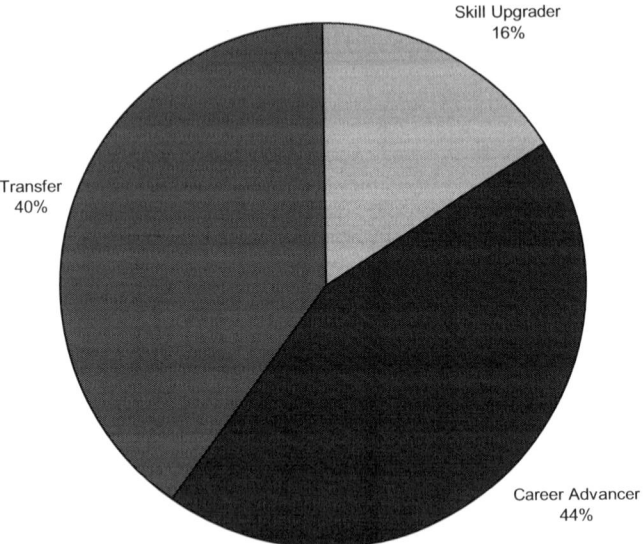

Figure 1. Three Major Categories of WCC Students

Table 3. Cluster Analysis Result: Nine-Cluster Profile of WCC Student Body (Study 1)

	Skill Upgraders		Career Advancers				Transfer		
	Cluster 1	Cluster 2	Cluster 3	Cluster 4	Cluster 5	Cluster 6	Cluster 7	Cluster 8	Cluster 9
	Personal Enrichment	Non-Traditional Students	Certificate for Work	Skills for Work	Degree for Computer Field	Degree for Other Field	Degree Trans to 4 Year	Non-Degree Trans to 4 Yr.	Trans to HS or CC
N	40	25	34	45	50	48	61	70	30
Cluster %	9.93%	6.20%	8.44%	11.17%	12.41%	11.91%	15.14%	17.37%	7.44%
Demographics									
Minority	6%	67%	9%	10%	15%	26%	19%	16%	18%
Female	30%	80%	50%	33%	52%	65%	54%	43%	70%
Over 25	95%	91%	59%	63%	66%	72%	13%	14%	17%
In District	90%	36%	65%	69%	84%	48%	80%	67%	67%
Previous Higher Ed	73%	79%	44%	53%	53%	67%	10%	43%	48%
Employed Full-Time	48%	32%	74%	69%	51%	69%	21%	43%	27%
Academic									
New Student	28%	88%	41%	62%	42%	44%	43%	61%	63%
>3.5 GPA	33%	68%	52%	40%	40%	57%	45%	58%	56%
Dual Enrollment	0%	0%	0%	7%	6%	4%	0%	1%	73%
Full-Time Enrollment	28%	20%	18%	31%	51%	17%	39%	26%	28%
Non Degree	87%	28%	0%	98%	0%	0%	0%	99%	100%
Associate's Degree	3%	12%	3%	3%	98%	100%	87%	0%	0%
Certificate	5%	56%	97%	5%	2%	0%	15%	0%	0%
BCT	8%	88%	15%	42%	92%	4%	25%	24%	0%
HAT	13%	4%	44%	9%	0%	58%	10%	17%	10%
MNB	18%	4%	9%	18%	6%	4%	23%	16%	3%
HSS	30%	4%	12%	16%	0%	29%	41%	31%	67%
Tech, Unspecified	33%	0%	18%	13%	2%	4%	2%	11%	0%
Talk to Faculty	48%	63%	38%	27%	38%	35%	53%	43%	23%
Reason For Enrolling									
Work	0%	36%	100%	98%	80%	96%	2%	0%	0%
Transfer	0%	0%	0%	0%	10%	2%	97%	99%	87%
Personal	98%	60%	0%	0%	10%	2%	2%	1%	7%
Also To Transfer to 4 Yr	5%	28%	12%	22%	30%	60%	93%	99%	3%

and had high GPAs (over 3.5) at the end of Fall 2001. These students tended to be taking courses related to clerical work and computer technology. Although most reported enrollment for personal reasons, some also reported work-related reasons. More of these students reported an intention to transfer to a four-year college than the Personal Enrichment students, even though both clusters had an equivalently high frequency of previous higher education.

Career Advancer Clusters

Although they had varying academic pursuits, the Career Advancers shared the desire to pursue a WCC education for employment purposes. They made up 44% of our total sample and included four clusters: Certificate for Work, Skills for Work, Degree for the Computer Field, and Degree for Other Programs. The specific programs were: Applied Technologies, Math, Natural and Behavioral Sciences, and Culinary Arts. Students in these clusters shared many of the characteristics that describe non-traditional students, including being employed in full-time work, over the age of 25, and enrolled part-time. Furthermore, 76% of all Career Advancers were enrolled in technology related programs, including BCT, HAT, or Technology unspecified (See Figure 2; refer to measures section for descriptions of program acronyms).

Cluster 3: Certificate for Work (8.4%). The students in the Certificate for Work cluster were those career advancers pursuing certificates, presumably to further their current careers, as the vast majority were employed full-time. Those in the graphic arts, child care, and applied technologies (such as automotive and welding) were well-represented in this cluster. These were students who seemed to be interested in supplementing their current careers with a certification, and very few intended to transfer credits to a four-year institution.

Cluster 4: Skills for Work (11.2%). Those in the Skills for Work cluster were mostly males. They were looking to gain skills related to their job and were largely non-degree students. This was a diverse cluster in terms of programs, with students fairly well represented among the clerical, applied technology, humanities/social science, computer, and medical fields. Overall, these students appeared to be those who came to WCC in order to supplement their knowledge of their current fields and to acquire career skills they may have been lacking.

Students in the next two clusters planned to earn associate's degrees for work-related purposes, but one cluster was overwhelmingly comprised of BCT students (92%) and the other cluster was primarily composed of students in HAT and HSS (58% and 29%, respectively).

Cluster 5: Degree for the Computer Field (12.4%). The Degree for the Computer field cluster was comprised of mostly in-district students, only half of whom were employed full-time. Of all of the Career Advancers, more students in this cluster were enrolled full-time, probably because fewer students in this cluster had full-time jobs. Overall, these students appeared to be students who wished to advance their current or new technology-related careers.

Cluster 6: Degree for Other Fields (11.9%) Culinary Arts, Applied Technologies, or Math, Natural and Behavioral Sciences Fields. More students in this cluster were female and/or minority students than any of the other Career Advancers. The majority of these students intended to transfer credits to four-year institutions, which was not the case for any of the other Career Advancers. These students appeared to be those who were employed full-time, enrolled part-time, and had a desire to attend community college, and perhaps continue to four-year institutions to advance their careers.

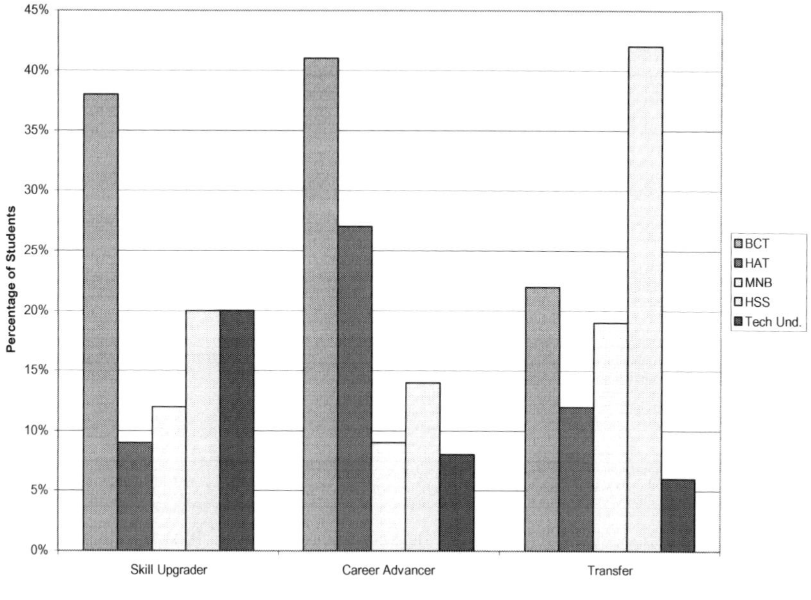

Transfer Student Clusters

In general, those who were in the Transfer Student clusters enrolled in WCC with the goal of transferring credits to other institutions. For the most part, students characterized as Transfer Students were the more traditional college students and they comprised 40% of the total sample. Eighty-six percent of all Transfer Students were un-

Figure 2. Academic Division by WCC Cluster Category

der the age of 25 (See Figure 3). Unlike the Career Advancers, a minority of the Transfer Students was employed full time (32%), and they were mainly concentrated in the humanities and social sciences (42%). Three distinct types were found in the Transfer Student category, including the Associate's Degree Transfer to Four Year, Non-Degree Transfer to Four Year, and Dual Enroll Transfer to High School or Community College.

Cluster 7: Degree to Transfer to Four Year (15.1%). Very few students in this cluster had previous higher education. In addition, it was unlikely for these students to be employed full-time, but more than a third were enrolled full-time. These students were enrolled in a wide range of fields, such as the humanities/social science, computers, business, applied technologies, graphic arts, and clerical areas. This cluster represents traditional college students who chose to first earn a degree at a community college before enrolling in a four-year institution.

Cluster 8: Non-Degree to Transfer to Four Year (17.4%). This cluster was similar to the previous cluster described, but these students were not pursuing degrees at the community college level. These students were more likely to have had previous higher education and to be employed full-time. A wide range of programs was represented in this cluster, including the humanities/social sciences, computer, business, math, natural and behavioral sciences, medical, applied technology, and child care fields. Overall, this cluster seemed to represent traditional college students who wished to experience college classes or explore their opportunities before transferring to four-year institutions.

Cluster 9: Dual Enroll to Transfer to High School or Community College (7.4%). This particular cluster consisted of students who were not pursuing degrees from WCC, however planned to transfer their credits, but not to four-year colleges or universities. The overwhelming majority of these Dual Enrolled Transfer students was simultaneously enrolled at a high school or another community college to which they wished to transfer their WCC credits. The majority of the students in this cluster were female, and many had previous (or simul-taneous) higher education experience. This was a small cluster with most being in the humanities and social sciences. However, students were also spread out among the computer, business, math, natural and behavioral sciences, applied technology, and medical disciplines.

Study 2: Method Validation

The second study was conducted in order to validate the methodology through replication, as well as to begin a longitudinal glimpse into gradual changes in our student body that may occur over time. A secondary reason was to determine how a change in our survey affected the results of our clusters. In Study 2 we inferred the student's educational goal through student records (at the time of application) rather than asking the student directly via the survey instrument.

Sample

The sample for this second analysis used responses from the 2002 CSS. In addition to survey responses from a random sample of 435 students, this study incorporated student data from the WCC institutional information system. The sample included degree and non-degree students from a wide variety of backgrounds and academic interests. About 47% of the survey respondents were female and 29% were students of color (African-American, Hispanic, Asian, Native American, or Other). Nearly two-thirds of the sample had previous higher education experience, almost half (42%) were employed full-time, and 32% were enrolled full-time. The sample was slightly more edu-

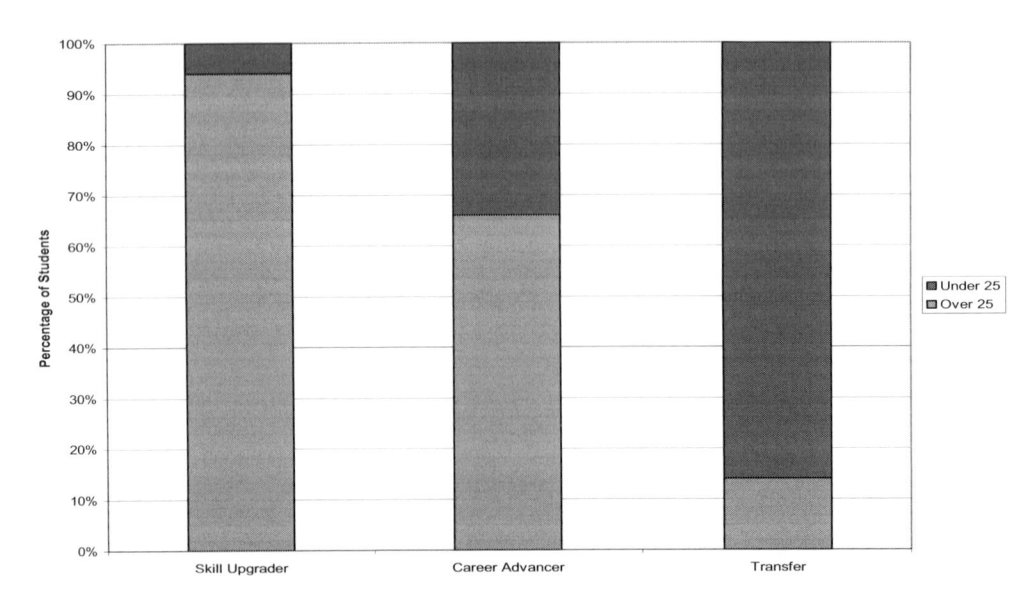

Figure 3. Age of Students by WCC Cluster Category

cated and included more new students than the total student body at WCC in Fall 2002. See Table 4 for more detailed descriptive sample data on key variables.

Measures

The variables of interest in this cluster analysis can be categorized into three major groups: demographic, academic, and educational goal. We transformed all categorical and continuous variables into dichotomous variables, as described in Study 1.

Demographic Variables. The first group of variables included in the analysis was a set of demographic variables that provided an idea of what backgrounds and life circumstances the students brought to WCC. Demographic variables of interest were: minority status (African- American, Hispanic, Asian, Native American, and Other), female, older student (age 25+), previous higher education (college graduates or transfers from other two- or four-year institutions), in-district (Washtenaw County), and employed full-time (30 hours or more per week).

Academic Variables. The second group consisted of academic-related variables that captured the students' academic status and interests at WCC. These included: high GPA (>3.5 at end of fall 2001); new student; study load (full-time/part-time); dual enrollment (currently enrolled at another institution—high school or college); non-degree; and academic program–Business and Communications Technology (BCT), Health and Applied Technology (HAT), Humanities and Social Science (HSS), Mathematics, Natural and Behavioral Sciences (MNB), or Technology non-degree.

Educational Goal. The final group of variables captured the students' intended goals or use of their WCC education. This question was *not* asked on the 2002 CSS; therefore, these data were collected from students' declared intentions in the college database. These included: work-related reasons, to transfer credits, for a degree, and for personal satisfaction. There was also a separate question on the CSS asking whether the student planned to transfer his or her credits.

Results for Study 2

In an attempt to replicate Study 1, we entered the same variables and specified a nine-cluster solution. Our final cluster solution in Study 2 identified nine useful student sub-bodies. As indicated by the high *F* values, the cluster formation was primarily driven by the student's educational goal and whether they enrolled non-degree or pursued a certificate or associate's degree (See Table 5 for *F* statistics). Demographic variables such as gender, race, residency, new-student status, and dual enrollment had lower *F* values, suggesting that they played less of a role in differentiating clusters. Age, however, was an important variable in this analysis.

Further analysis of the specific characteristics of each cluster revealed two primary categories into which these clusters fall: *Career/Skill Advances* and *Transfer Students* (See Figure 4). We suspect that only two major categories were revealed in this analysis because, unlike Study 1, Study 2 only analyzed students' intent as expressed officially in their enrollment data. In Study 2, students were not asked the primary reason for enrolling at WCC in the distributed survey.

Table 4. Descriptive Statistics of Survey Respondents (2002) Compared to Overall WCC Student Body

Characteristic	Sample Percent (*n* = 435)	Overall WCC % (*N* = 11,746)
Minority	29	30
Female	47	56
Over 25	46	46
In District	62	69
Previous Higher Education	67	43
New-Student Status	45	29
Full-Time Enrollment	32	27
Non-Degree	31	30

Career/Skill Advancer 33%
Transfer 67%

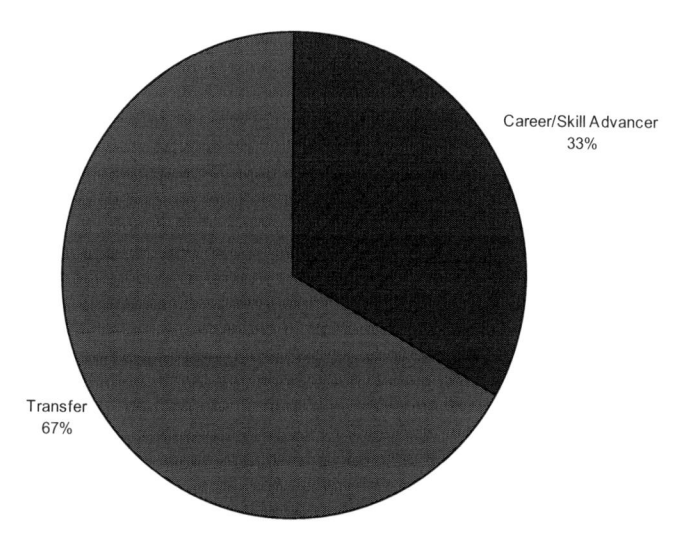

Figure 4. Two Major Categories of WCC Students

Table 5. One-Way Analysis of Variance Results for Nine-Cluster Solution

Demographics	Between Cluster Mean Square	Within Cluster Mean Square	F
Minority	0.335	0.202	1.660
Female	1.636	0.224	7.307
Over 25	5.352	0.151	35.338
In District	0.692	0.227	3.051
Previous Higher Ed	1.232	0.198	6.225
Employed Full-Time	1.561	0.220	7.101
Academic			
New-Student Status	0.542	0.243	2.234
>3.5 GPA	2.519	0.200	12.566
Dual Enrollment	0.101	0.091	1.111
Full-Time Enrollment	2.307	0.178	12.972
Non-Degree	10.476	0.022	480.323
Associate's Degree	12.371	0.021	585.735
Certificate	4.537	0.043	105.678
BCT	3.382	0.164	20.602
HAT	1.969	0.150	13.127
MNB	0.269	0.134	2.002
HSS	1.654	0.152	10.865
Tech, Unspecified	0.020	0.025	0.819
Primary Reason For Enrolling			
For Job	0.002	0.002	1.033
For Transfer	9.298	0.080	115.962
For Personal Interest	0.004	0.005	0.907
For Degree	12.032	0.014	832.642
Transfer to 4 Year	2.546	0.200	12.735

Career/Skill Advancer Clusters

In general, Career and Skill Advancers were those students who enrolled in WCC in order to increase their skills and knowledge for job-related or personal reasons. Students characterized as Career and Skill Advancers made up 33% of the total sample. This category consisted of four clusters: Skills for Work; Degree for the Computer & Business Fields; Degree for the Applied Technologies, Humanities & Social Sciences, or Math, Natural & Behavioral Sciences Fields; and Certificate for Career.

This category included a mixture of degree, certificate, and non-degree students. Overall, the Career and Skill Advancers were those with previous higher education experience prior to enrolling at WCC and enrolled for their careers, personal interests, or reasons other than transfer (See Table 6).

Table 6. Cluster Analysis Result: Nine Cluster Profile of WCC Student Body (Study 2)

	Career/Skill Advancers					Transfer			
	Cluster 1	Cluster 2	Cluster 3	Cluster 4	Cluster 5	Cluster 6	Cluster 7	Cluster 8	Cluster 9
	Skills for Work	Degree for Computer/ Business	Degree for Other Field	Certificate for Career	Non-Degree, Developed Interest	Non-Degree for Transfer	Certificate for Transfer	Degree, Developed Interest	Degree for Transfer
N	51	29	37	27	47	47	17	62	118
Cluster %	11.72%	6.67%	8.51%	6.21%	10.80%	10.80%	3.91%	14.25%	27.13%
Demographics									
Minority	22%	41%	16%	19%	26%	38%	41%	36%	26%
Female	51%	38%	46%	48%	75%	4%	47%	48%	54%
Over 25	94%	89%	83%	52%	6%	30%	63%	2%	47%
In District	86%	41%	65%	71%	68%	51%	59%	55%	61%
Previous Higher Ed	90%	76%	89%	67%	43%	57%	88%	52%	71%
Employed Full-Time	75%	76%	46%	48%	30%	30%	35%	24%	38%
Academic									
New Student	47%	38%	46%	15%	45%	60%	41%	55%	42%
>3.5 GPA	78%	60%	77%	22%	22%	36%	80%	20%	36%
Dual Enrollment	6%	0%	14%	11%	15%	6%	18%	8%	13%
Full-Time Enrollment	4%	3%	8%	22%	57%	51%	29%	60%	28%
Non Degree	94%	0%	0%	0%	94%	92%	0%	0%	0%
Associate's Degree	0%	83%	100%	0%	0%	0%	0%	97%	98%
Certificate	6%	17%	0%	100%	6%	8%	100%	3%	2%
BCT	39%	97%	0%	7%	6%	68%	24%	29%	33%
HAT	30%	0%	57%	74%	15%	6%	6%	13%	25%
MNB	10%	0%	24%	15%	26%	23%	6%	19%	14%
HSS	16%	3%	16%	0%	53%	2%	65%	36%	24%
Tech, Unspecified	6%	0%	3%	4%	0%	0%	0%	3%	3%
Reason For Enrolling									
For Job	0%	0%	0%	0%	2%	0%	0%	0%	0%
For Transfer	67%	0%	0%	11%	38%	72%	0%	0%	100%
For Personal Interest	0%	0%	0%	0%	2%	2%	0%	0%	0%
For Degree	0%	100%	100%	85%	0%	0%	88%	98%	0%
Plan To Transfer 4 Yr	26%	35%	38%	41%	87%	66%	71%	90%	57%

Furthermore, these students tended to be over the age of 25, and many were employed full-time. These students were mainly studying health and applied technologies or business and computer technologies (See Figure 5).

Cluster 1: Skills for Work (11.7%). About 12% of the students surveyed fell into the Skills for Work cluster. These students were overwhelmingly over the age of 25. Three-quarters of these students were employed full-time, and almost all of these students had some previous higher education. Skills for Work students majored in a wide variety of areas, including computers, business, clerical, applied technologies, and graphic arts. The vast majority (94%) of these students were not pursuing a degree at WCC. Although many declared that they originally intended on transferring their credits, at the time of the survey only 26% of the students claimed that they wanted to transfer credits. Therefore, it may be inferred by the applied nature of their majors and their work status that these students were gaining skills needed for their careers, similar to Cluster 4 in Study 1.

Cluster 2: Degree for Computer/Business (6.7%). Of all of the Career/Skill Advancers, the Degree for Computer/Business cluster had the most minority students and the fewest from in-district (41% for both categories). Again, about three-quarters of these students were employed full time, and 89% were over the age of 25. Most had some previous higher education. These students tended to be taking courses related to business and computer technology. All of these students declared that their educational goal was degree attainment, and only about one-third had intentions to transfer credits. Eighty-three percent of these students were working toward an associate's degree, whereas 17% were working toward a certificate. This cluster was most similar to Cluster 5 in Study 1.

Cluster 3: Degree for Other Programs (8.5%) The Applied Technologies, Humanities & Social Sciences, or Math, Natural and Behavioral Sciences Fields. The students in this cluster tended to be over the age of 25 and had some previous higher education (83% and 89%, respectively). Only about half were employed full-time, but all declared that they were enrolling for an associate's degree. Again, only a minority of students intended to transfer credits, suggesting that they were earning their degrees to begin or advance their careers. This cluster resembled Cluster 6 in Study 1.

Cluster 4: Certificate for Career (6.2%). Only about half of these students were over the age of 25. Of the Career/Skill Advancers, this cluster had the fewest students employed full-time or with previous higher education (48% and 67%, respectively). The majority of these students were returning students to WCC. All of these students were pursuing a certificate, and 85% declared they enrolled to earn a degree. These students were mainly taking courses in the applied technologies, child care, and medical fields. This cluster was similar to Cluster 3 in Study 1.

Transfer Student Clusters

In general, those who were in the Transfer Student clusters enrolled in WCC with the goal of transferring credits to another institution. For the most part, students characterized as Transfer Students were the more traditional college students and they comprised 67% of the total sample. Seventy-one percent of all Transfer Students were under the age of 25 (See Figure 6). Unlike the Career Advancers, fewer of these students were employed full-time (64% vs. 80%) and more were in the humanities and social sciences fields (Figure 5). Five distinct types were found in the Transfer Student category, including the Non-Degree, Developed Interest; Non-Degree for Transfer; Certificate for Transfer; Degree, Developed Interest; and Degree for Transfer.

Cluster 5: Non-Degree, Developed Interest in Transfer (10.8%). A minority of students in this cluster had previous higher education experience (43%). In addition, it was unlikely for these students to be employed full-time, but over half were enrolled at WCC full-time. These students were enrolled in mainly the humanities and social sciences, child care, and medical studies. The majority was not pursuing a degree at WCC (94%) and was female (75%). Almost all were under the age of 25. Less than half of the students surveyed had declared a goal on

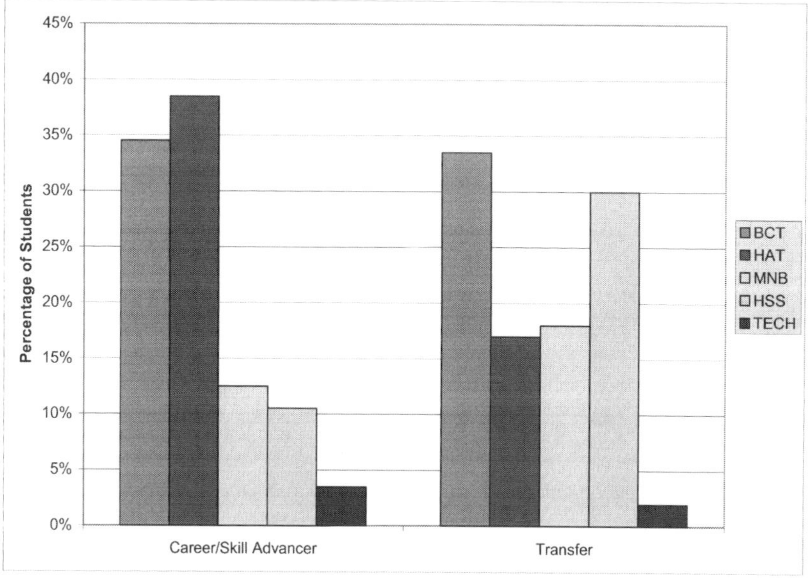

Figure 5. Academic Division by WCC Cluster Category

his/her application, but the vast majority (87%) when surveyed planned on transferring. This suggests that these students may have enrolled at WCC to "get their feet wet" before deciding whether to enter the workforce or continue their education, but eventually decided that a four-year education was the path they wanted to pursue. This cluster was unique to Study 2, as no parallel cluster existed in Study 1.

Cluster 6: Non-Degree for Transfer (10.8%). This cluster was similar to the previous cluster described, but these students had intended to transfer all along. Ninety-two percent were non-degree students at WCC. Most of these students were male, had previous higher education, and were new students at WCC. A wide range of programs was represented in this cluster, including computer technology, business, math, natural and behavioral sciences, and graphic arts. Overall, this cluster seemed to represent traditional college students who wished to take non-credit college courses before beginning at a four-year institution. This cluster was similar to Cluster 8 in Study 1.

Cluster 7: Certificate for Transfer (3.9%). This particular cluster consisted of certificate students who planned to transfer to four-year colleges or universities. Although their original intention was to get a certificate (88%), 71% of these students had reported when surveyed that they wanted to transfer. This cluster was composed of students predominantly over the age of 25, setting them apart from the other transfer clusters. The Certificate for Transfer cluster contained the most students with high GPAs. The success of students in this cluster may have accounted for their change in intention to continue at another institution. This was a small cluster with most being in the humanities and social sciences. This cluster was unique to Study 2, as no parallel cluster existed in Study 1.

Cluster 8: Degree, Developed Interest in Transfer (14.3%). These students were similar to Cluster 5 above, in that they originally enrolled for reasons other than transfer. However, by the time of the survey, 90% reported that they wanted to transfer to a four-year institution. The vast majority (98%) of these students was under 25, and few were employed full-time. Sixty percent were enrolled full time at WCC. These students demonstrated a wide range of interests, including enrollment in humanities, social sciences, business, computers, mathematics, and natural and behavioral sciences courses. This cluster was unique to Study 2, as no parallel cluster existed in Study 1.

Cluster 9: Degree for Transfer (27.1%). This cluster consisted of associate's degree students, 100% of whom enrolled with the intent to transfer. Seventy-one percent had previous higher education. These students pursued a range of coursework, including enrollment in humanities, social sciences, business, applied technologies, medical, and graphic arts classes. This cluster was similar to Cluster 7 in Study 1.

Conclusions

Cluster analysis of background characteristics, academic choices, and intent of the WCC student body can help community college researchers, administrators, and staff better understand their diversifying student populations. The profiles of various sub-populations provided a systematic basis toward understanding and meeting students' varying developmental, social, educational, and occupational needs.

For the most part, in Study 1 clusters were formed according to students' educational goals. This supported VanDerLinden's (2002) choice to focus on this as a key descriptive variable at the community college level. However, other important distinctions emerged as well. The Skill Upgrader clusters had prior educational experience, were older, and enrolled for mainly personal reasons. Within this category, a Personal Enrichment cluster emerged, which included in-district students taking culinary arts, graphic arts, and business courses for their own

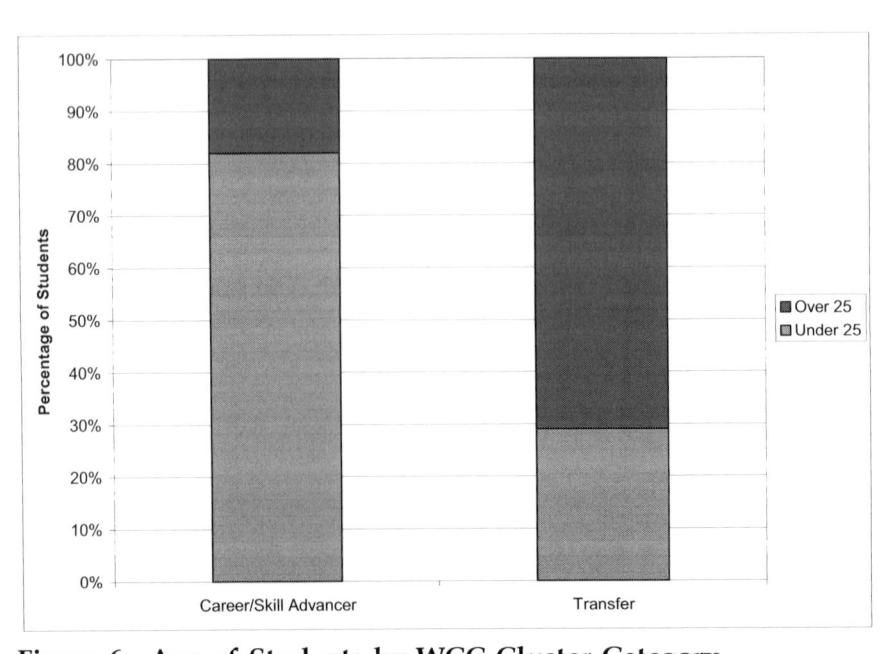

Figure 6. Age of Students by WCC Cluster Category

enjoyment. The Non-Traditional Students were different, in that the majority of these students were new to WCC, female, minorities, and traveling to WCC from-out-of district. These students also tended to be enrolled in clerical and computer courses.

The Career Advancer clusters were highly likely to be enrolled for work-related reasons, were older, and likely to be employed full time. For the most part, these students further clustered according to whether they were earning a certificate, associate's degree, or were non-credit students. Also, division and intent to transfer played a role in driving these clusters.

Finally, the Transfer clusters were those students who indicated intent to transfer credits to another institution. These clusters were further distinguished according to whether they were degree students. Also, the type of institution (four-year or two-year college or high school) to which the students planned to transfer was influential in forming these clusters. These clusters were mainly composed of those considered to be traditional college students.

Study 2 served as a fairly good validation of Study 1. Six of the nine clusters (Skills for Work, Degree for Computer/Business, Degree for Other Field, Certificate for Career, Non-Degree for Transfer, and Degree for Transfer) overlapped with those in Study 1. However, Study 1 uniquely had two personal interest clusters, as well as a cluster of dually enrolled high school students. Three unique transfer student groups emerged in Study 2:

(1) non-degree students who decided after some time at WCC that they intended to transfer to a four year institutions,
(2) degree students who after some time at WCC decided that their goal was to transfer to a four-year institution, and
(3) certificate students who intended to transfer to a four-year institution.

It could be that the Fall 2002 cohort differed from the Fall 2001 cohort, in that more students with different "stories" intended to transfer to four year institutions. However, students in the Fall 2002 cohort were not asked the main reason for getting their degrees on the CSS. Therefore, if students intended to transfer, there is no way to know if that was truly the *main* reason for their education at WCC. Future analyses should insure that the same questions are used in the cluster analysis, in order to maintain consistency when comparing student profiles over time.

Also, Study 2 identified the difficulty of maintaining accurate records of student intent. Although students at some point may have declared an educational goal for their degree, which is stored in the college information system, students' intentions change over time and they often fail to update their educational goal officially with the college. Furthermore, only 3 of the 435 students indicated that they enrolled for their jobs or personal interest, although this is almost certainly inaccurate. As 48% of students indicated that they were at WCC for purposes of transferring, and 38% indicated that they were at WCC for a degree, it appears that for some reason these are the two options students are most likely to choose. Perhaps students are advised most often to choose one of these options, or perhaps the other options have for some reason become obsolete and over time not used. Future research should look into the usefulness of educational goals in the college system and consider ways of maintaining the accuracy of this information.

Overall, it is interesting to note that academic variables were more important in categorizing students than were background variables such as race and gender. This is encouraging because it suggests that those who are traditionally considered at-risk for academic difficulties are not clustering together in predictable ways. Future longitudinal cluster analyses should be conducted to see if clustering changes over time.

Cluster analysis is a tool that can help stakeholders understand the range of students they are serving at the community college. Our own analysis demonstrates how cluster analysis can be used as a snapshot of a student body at one point in time. Using cluster analysis to characterize incoming students each term can assist administrators and educators in seeing how new student groups differ from previous cohorts of students.

Once clusters are established, membership can be used to predict different types of successes and failures at the community college and beyond. In addition, future research should incorporate additional data about the use of different student services and student impressions of these services. Cluster analyses that include these types of data will provide more thorough evaluations of the students who are more likely to use certain services, students who find the services helpful, and students who may be left out. It is very possible that different types of students have different experiences on the community college campus; further analysis of our own data will help us detect if that is the case at WCC. By using clusters as predictors in an analysis of service usage, researchers and administrators should be able to improve student services initiatives and ensure they are properly serving and marketing to all members of a diverse student body.

References

Aldenderfer, M. S., & Blashfield, R. K. (1984). *Cluster Analysis.* Newbury Park, CA: Sage Publications.

Andrews, H. A. (2003). Enrollment trends in community colleges. *ERIC Digest, 2003-05-00,* ED477914.

Boughan, K. (2000). The role of academic process in student achievement: An application of structural equations modeling and cluster analysis to community college longitudinal data. *AIR Professional File, 74,* 1-17.

Bryant, A. N. (2001). Community college students: Recent findings and trends. *Community College Review, 29,* 77-93.

Phipps, R. A., Shedd, J. M., Merisotis, J. P., & Carroll, C. D. (2001). A classification system for 2-year postsecondary institutions. *National Center for Education Statistics Methodology Report: Postsecondary Education Descriptive Analysis Reports.* NCES 2001-167.

Schuetz, P. (2002). Emerging challenges for community colleges. *ERIC Digest, 2002-08-00,* ED477829.

VanDerLinden, K. (2002). Credit student analysis: 1999 and 2000. *American Association of Community Colleges, Faces of the Future: A Portrait of America's Community College Students, 2002-04-00.* Washington, DC: AACC.

Bridget V. Ammon *is a doctoral candidate in the Combined Program of Education and Psychology at the University of Michigan and holds an M.A. in psychology from Marywood University.*

Jamillah Bowman *is a law student at Stanford University and holds an M.A. from the Center for Study of Higher and Postsecondary Education at the University of Michigan.*

Roger Mourad, *Ph.D., J.D., is the Director of Institutional Research at Washtenaw Community College. He can be contacted at* mou@wccnet.org.

Peer Grouping: The Refinement of Performance Indicators

Willard Hom
Chancellor's Office, California Community Colleges.

Community colleges operate under much scrutiny these days, and these institutions have experienced a growing emphasis on performance indicators as paths to institutional accountability. California's system of 109 community colleges recently developed and implemented an innovative accountability program that used peer group comparison as one of its elements. This article describes California's use of peer grouping in terms of its development, mechanics, and implications for the future.

Introduction

For purposes of evaluation and planning, higher education institutions have often tried to compare themselves to other institutions on selected performance indicators. This common practice gives college officials some idea of "where their institutions stand" with respect to a certain performance indicator. But college officials generally recognize that such a comparison is only valid and fair if it involves colleges with similar characteristics. In fact, the Integrated Postsecondary Education Data System (IPEDS) tries to address this historic need by integrating a "peer selection" procedure on its website (US Department of Education, 2007). The Carnegie Foundation has provided a framework for identifying peer institutions since 1970 (Carnegie, 2007; McCormick & Zhao, 2005). A study from the National Center for Educational Statistics (NCES) actually identified groups of similar colleges through a cluster analysis of various postsecondary institutions in the U.S. (Phipps, et al., 2001) and a new analysis extends that work (Goan & Cunningham, 2007). The National Survey of Student Engagement (NSSE) system has attempted to help an institution to find its institutional peers in its data system (National Survey of Student Engagement, 2007). Finally, one publisher even devoted an entire volume of its series to the topic of peer identification (McCormick & Cox, 2003). Hurley (2002) documents the various efforts that have focused upon finding peer institutions for community colleges.

Postsecondary educational institutions have company when it comes to this need to compare themselves for evaluative purposes. California's secondary education system essentially administers its accountability program, with its Academic Performance Index (API), in such a way that each school's performance has a set of similar schools (its "peers") to facilitate a fair comparison (California Department of Education, 2007).

In any case, to determine which institution is a "similar school" in the postsecondary environment, an analyst can undertake an extensive analysis to categorize or classify a specific population into groups so that each group contains institutions that closely resemble one another. Researchers often label such an analysis as *peer grouping*. Researchers use peer grouping to "level the playing field" or to avoid the problem of "comparing apples to oranges." In essence, peer grouping is a method of arranging data so that people can compare institutions while "controlling" for specific, measured factors (often referred to as "confounders") that would otherwise lead to unfair and invalid comparisons of performance.

How California Constructed Its Peer Grouping

California used peer grouping to satisfy an assortment of legislative, political, and technical criteria. California's central office for the state's 109 community colleges (henceforth known as the System Office) had responsibility for implementing state-level mandates that affect these institutions. The System Office therefore had authority to plan and implement a peer grouping plan that the state legislature had passed in 2004 (Chancellor's Office, 2007).

Historically, state oversight bodies (such as the California Department of Finance and the Legislative Analyst's Office) have preferred straightforward forms of evaluation such as institutional rankings. Rankings can give analysts quick, if simple, insights into relative performances of institutions. When the rankings involve a rate or proportion for each institution, this form of performance reporting provides busy oversight bodies with the most familiar and useful type of policy-making information. On the other hand, college officials have argued that their missions are so complex that any single numeric performance indicator will fail to give a valid and fair portrayal of their institutional performance. These officials hold that performance indicators must account for the different environments of each institution (i.e., the kind of students enrolled and their proximity to receiving transfer institutions, et al.), the limited accuracy and coverage of administrative data, and unique historical events (i.e., natural disasters and relevant policy changes, et al.) before policy makers and local voters can take these indicators seriously. At the same time, most college officials face a dilemma with two major elements. They have scarce resources with which to develop the data and analysis systems to fulfill the aforesaid requirements of performance indicators, and they tend to lack the background in evaluation research to envision a methodological solution that can satisfy the public's demand for performance rankings. In this situation, the System Office for the community colleges developed a peer grouping approach that largely satisfied the needs and interests of these two political groups: oversight bodies and college officials. To a large extent, the peer grouping approach also served the mission of the System Office. It found a "middle ground" that allowed the oversight agencies to understand community college performance in new and objective ways while capturing much of the diversity in institutional environments and institutional missions. This compromise (a) promoted the chances of improved funding from the Governor's Office and the Legislature and (b) fortified the System Office's role as a problem-solving go-between in the community college scene—two strategic goals for the state agency responsible for helping to manage the state's higher education system.

The state's current effort at accountability, known as Accountability Reporting for the Community Colleges (ARCC), emerged from the demise of a program known as the Partnership for Excellence (PFE). Beginning in 1998, the PFE program acted as a first step toward accountability in the state system, but oversight bodies showed dissatisfaction with its limited analyses (Legislative Analyst's Office, 2007). Although the state leadership chose to abandon PFE, much of the basic data collection mechanisms and concepts for performance indicators eventually served as foundations for the ARCC performance indicators.

To identify the members of a particular peer group, the researcher can apply a variety of classification methods but a statistical method known as *cluster analysis* has often been the tool of choice (Everitt, et al., 2001; Lorr, 1987). In disciplines such as business, medicine/public health, psychology, and political science, researchers have historically applied cluster analysis to obtain peer groupings. Hurley (2002) discusses how cluster analysis, among other methods, has been employed in various community college peer grouping efforts.

Cluster analysis has a number of advantages and disadvantages that the System Office considered before it chose this method as its tool for classifying the colleges into groups for comparison. One critical advantage that this quantitative tool had over subjective tools (such as a jury of expert opinion for a reputation-based classification) is the capacity of cluster analysis to prevent politically biased peer grouping that would favor certain colleges. Table 1 displays the advantages and disadvantages of this method for the System Office. The advantages and disadvantages in Table 1 are really general considerations. Cluster analysis has a decisive technical advantage over other quantitative classification methods or data mining tools in that the user can proceed despite the lack of any information about the "true group membership" for each entity in the population under study (Han & Kamber, 2001). In the case of California's community colleges, there is no way to identify the true group membership of each

Table 1. Advantages and Disadvantages of Cluster Analysis

	Advantage	Disadvantage
1	Many institutional researchers have a familiarity with it (it is not an alien concept).	Lay audiences feel it is very complex (giving it a "black box" image).
2	Most researchers can learn to use or understand it even without much prior exposure to it.	Its results can vary noticeably if the analyst uses different clustering options (i.e., with some datasets results may not be robust).
3	Most major statistical programs implement it (so replication is easy).	Its results impart the appearance of precision and clear differences when true differences may be fuzzy.
4	It has use and acceptance in many different fields of research (therefore established legitimacy as an analytical tool).	It can produce results that appear counter-intuitive to audiences who have formed personal judgments of their peer institutions.
5	It has flexibility to meet user needs (i.e., users can adapt the tool to their analytical situations).	Its resulting groups may be difficult to "validate."
6	Its "transparent" usage in peer groupings limits the potential for analyst bias and suspicion of favoritism.	Its results tend to depend upon esoteric methods to graph groups (visually display), such as the dendrogram.

institution.

The most notable technical disadvantage of cluster analysis is that "it is difficult to tell whether a cluster analysis has been successful. Contrast this with predictive modeling, in which we can take a test data set and see how accurately the value of the target variable is predicted in this set. Generally speaking, the validity of a clustering is often in the eye of the beholder; for example, if a cluster produces an interesting scientific insight, we can judge it to be useful. Quantifying this precisely is difficult, if not impossible, since the interpretation of how interesting a clustering is will inevitably be application-dependent and subjective to some degree..." (Hand, Mannila, & Smyth, 2001).

The recent experience with peer grouping in ARCC may offer the analyst in other states some guidance. One major development in California's peer grouping project was the decision to give each community college a separate peer group for each performance indicator. As a result, the 2007 ARCC report produced a total of six peer groupings (one for each of the six performance indicators that had sufficient data in 2007). This policy recognized the reality of the multiple missions that the public expects its colleges to perform. Research has shown that the system's community colleges do tend to specialize to some degree in the missions that they strive to achieve, making it misleading and unfair to evaluate such institutions on the basis of a single performance indicator (Gill & Leigh, 2004). Bailey (2003) pointed out, "Community college administrators and faculty articulate several central college missions, including granting degrees, transfer, workforce development, worker upgrading, and remediation...No strong consensus has emerged that identifies one or two central purposes of the community college..."

Development of the peer groups for each indicator went through specific steps (variable selection, regression modeling, and cluster analysis). Figure 1 shows the work flow that the ARCC project used for peer grouping through cluster analysis. The steps of literature review, field input, and review of COMIS (the System Office's database of community college data) functioned as a variable search/definition process. These steps occurred simultaneously in order to meet the schedule of the oversight agencies. The System Office planned for these steps to conclude before its analysis moved to the next step (the search for correlation), and each step could have used a different analyst operating independently of other analysts if needed.

In the search for the correlation step, the System Office executed a number of sub-steps. In the first sub-step, there was an *exploratory data analysis* or EDA (Mosteller & Tukey 1977). The EDA helped the System Office to decide which potential peer grouping variables had inadequate data quality to contribute to the prediction of a performance indicator. The prevalence of missing values and unrealistic distributions of values helped to establish the usability of specific variables. The extent of missing values had a decisive weight in the usability of a variable. If there were too many missing values in a variable, the peer group analysis either had to exclude some colleges from the peer grouping effort or use imputed values in place of the missing values. Omission of a college from the peer grouping would amount to excusing that college from the project's form of accountability for a particular performance indicator. On the other hand, imputation of missing values would have created a debate about the validity of a college's peer group membership. The EDA sub-step also helped to determine the need for possible data transformations of variables before testing for linear correlation (the next step).

The second sub-step, the actual search for correlation, tested for a bivariate relationship between each peer grouping variable and each performance indicator. This sub-step used scatter plots and correlation coefficients to judge association. For a robust test for bivariate correlation, the analysis used Spearman rank correlation coefficients, as well as the standard Pearson correlation coefficients. These tools helped staff to decide which data elements or variables to drop from further analysis. This screening of variables enabled the peer grouping effort to concentrate on a parsimonious set of variables. The bivariate correlations also helped the next step, the regression model, by

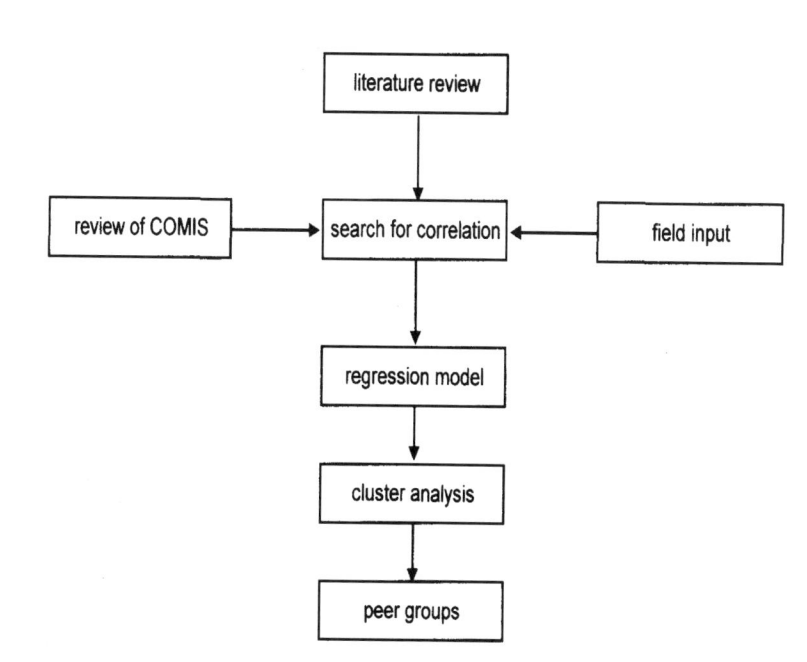

Figure 1. Steps in Formulation of Peer Groups

helping to identify potential instances of multicollinearity.

The next step in Figure 1 used ordinary least squares regression to find the best set of variables that predicted a performance indicator. This step aimed at identifying those variables that had a statistical relationship to a performance indicator and a theoretical connection from a causal perspective. Consequently, staff identified the fewest number of variables and the most "valid" variables for the ensuing step of cluster analysis. This is important for two reasons. (1) The analyst should only attempt to group colleges according to environmental factors that have an empirical and a theoretical relationship with a performance indicator, and (2) the cluster analysis will have more clarity (or transparency) if it uses the fewest number of variables possible. In the regression modeling, staff employed a standard regression analysis procedure that has been detailed elsewhere (Chancellor's Office, 2007). When staff completed this step, it had a small number of variables for use in the next step, cluster analysis.

In the cluster analysis step, staff needed to weigh the specific criteria that applied to California's accountability program. First of all, the System Office designed the peer grouping so that a college could belong to a different peer group for a different performance indicator as a means to achieve valid comparisons. So, the number of cluster analyses that the System Office conducted equaled the number of performance indicators that it was mandated to analyze. The state's oversight agencies sought comparison colleges for each college in the system. If a college had no comparison colleges, that is, if it had a peer group containing only itself, then that college essentially escaped accountability for its result on a specific performance indicator. So, the cluster analysis needed to minimize the occurrence of one-member peer groups. (To a lesser extent, the cluster analysis also needed to have few, if any, peer groups with only two or three members in them.) In some respects, the criterion for a minimum of small peer groups forced the System Office to create some peer groups that joined some colleges that would have been classified as different (i.e., relatively dissimilar) enough to appear as "outliers" in the system. The need to avoid too many instances of one-college peer groups related to another criterion for the peer grouping. The peer groups needed to divide the population of colleges so that the size of the groups did not become too large. That is, the System Office needed to avoid the creation of a peer group that contained a disproportionate number of the colleges. This criterion implements the notion that equal-sized groups would provide more equitable comparison situations than peer groups that had dramatically different numbers of colleges within them. In order to achieve these criteria, the System Office applied the Ward's method of clustering along with a target number of six clusters (so that approximately six groups of eighteen colleges per group would result). The System Office clustering also used two other options in the cluster analysis for each peer grouping. Staff standardized each clustering variable (i.e., each predictor from the regression model for a performance indicator) so that different scales of measurement would have no effect on the clustering. Secondly, staff chose the *hierarchical clustering* method so that the process of the group formation could be examined for sensitivity. Standard references on cluster analysis explain these clustering options. (Everitt, et al., 2001; Hair & Black, 2000; Lorr, 1987; Aldenderfer and Blashfield, 1984).

How Peer Groups Were Used

The preceding section covered the process that led to the construction of the peer groups. In this section the applications of the peer groupings are summarized. These applications largely embody the political and administrative issues that precipitated the mandate for the ARCC. Figure 2 below outlines the major elements involved in the application of the peer groups. The diagram basically displays the time sequence of the elements. After the System Office completed its peer groupings, colleges received a draft report containing these results as well as a wide array of related performance data. Each college used this draft information for its different performance indicators (including how these results compared to the results of its peer groups) to write a "self-assessment." This self-assessment provided the college's perspective on the reported results—essentially creating a formal way for colleges to offer explanations or responses to findings in the ARCC

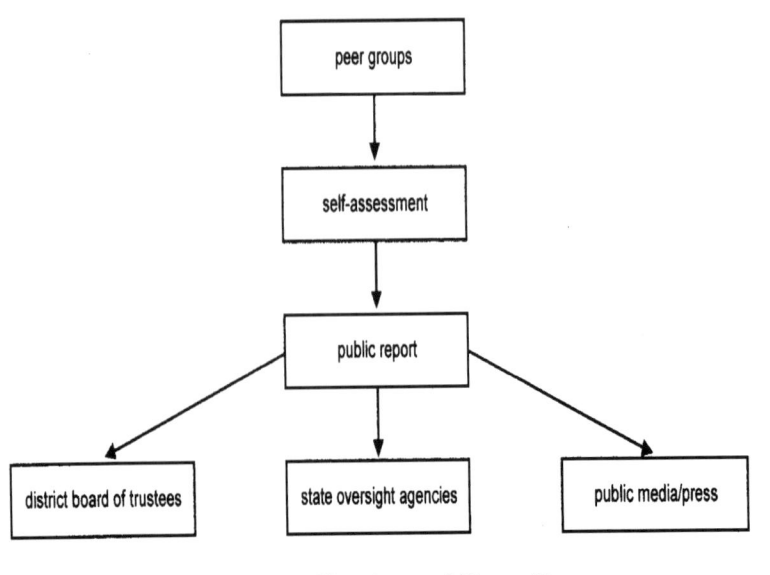

Figure 2. Steps in Application of Peer Groups

report.

Each college then submitted its self-assessment to the System Office, which incorporated these brief narratives into the final ARCC report. The final ARCC report then became available to the public through the System Office website, satisfying the legislation that mandated the ARCC project. However, release of the public report did not signify the last step in the ARCC process (and application of the peer grouping information).

The bottom three boxes of Figure 2 denote the three major actors who used the peer grouping information in the public report. The elected Board of Trustees for each community college district had to "interact" with the ARCC report and the peer grouping information. Within one year of the report's release, each district had to submit documentation of board interaction to the System Office. Through this process, local elected officials were expected to hold local college officials accountable for their performance. The peer groupings aided in board evaluations of college performance because they provided trustees a direct comparison of the local college to other colleges with similar challenges for a particular performance indicator — a tool that they hitherto had lacked. State oversight agencies applied the peer grouping information in the public report to their policy formulation and budget decisions. Although state oversight agencies did not use the ARCC report to attempt specific interventions within one or more districts, they did employ the report's peer group information as part of a general diagnosis of the system's performance. Last, but not least, the public media and press used the peer group information in the public report to alert the community to the shortcomings or strengths of their local institutions. The legislation that required the peer grouping does not mention the public media and press, but there is obvious value in helping communities to receive information that may help them to initiate local change (such as change in college policy or college personnel or local bond measures). In a sense, the public media/press acted here as part of a local accountability mechanism without direction (or funding) from the state government. Although Figure 2 omits a block at the bottom level for college officials (i.e., college presidents, vice-chancellors, and deans), we note that this group of actors began their application of the peer grouping in an earlier stage, the self-assessment stage, and this group will probably continue to apply that information throughout the year as college-based planning evolves.

Discussion

California's use of peer grouping had innovative qualities in both its methodological dimension and its administrative dimension. The use of a regression model to identify environmental factors for each performance indicator, in concert with a cluster analysis that used those environmental factors to define a peer group for each performance indicator, marks a milestone in community college accountability analysis. The integration of state-level indicators with college-level indicators, the use of four different perspectives of overall community college performance, and the breadth of the indicators also helped to distinguish California's implementation of peer grouping (Chancellor's Office, 2007). The integration of a technical advisory group, a college self-assessment, a web-based public report, the dissemination of peer grouping data and methods, and the requirement for local board interaction all set examples for future peer group applications in other states. The dissemination of the peer group data and methods, along with opportunities to submit corrected data, reinforced the System Office's efforts to ensure a valid and equitable accountability process. A number of colleges actually used the System Office-supplied "peer group toolbox" to replicate the peer group results that appeared in the public report.

California's early experience with peer grouping demonstrates the dynamics of accountability that can evolve from the inherently political nature of performance measurement and reporting. Peer grouping also creates a dilemma for college officials who must interact with different types of stakeholders. For an audience of accountability officials who focus upon the relative performance within a peer group, the names of the peer group colleges have fairly low relevance. For this audience, a college would probably prefer to have peer group members who have relatively weak performance records. On the other hand, a college will tend to prefer high-performing (i.e., high reputation) colleges as peer group partners if it needs to impress its local community especially the voting public, employers of its alumni, and potential students.

Analysts who face a "high stakes" accountability situation, inadequate data, insufficient staffing, or strong opposition to performance reporting may expect more difficulties in trying to use California's approach to peer grouping. The peer grouping implementation in California enjoyed a conducive environment. The legislation for ARCC did not tie the results to funding or direct repercussions such as heightened restrictions and authorized special staffing to implement the new accountability project. California has progressed far in its development of a comprehensive data system. Furthermore, the initial legislation allowed for time and a panel of experts to plan a system of accountability. Although various officials at the colleges voiced opposition to the accountability initiative (and to the peer grouping), this opposition did not expand into an organized effort of non-compliance or for counteractive legislation. Probably the most frequent hurdle in the peer grouping process was the difficulty that some college officials had in accepting peer groupings that associated their colleges with institutions that they had not traditionally viewed as peers. This difficulty appeared to occur most often with respect to peer colleges that had different geographic characteristics, different overall enrollment characteristics, or different public images.

In the planning of the ARCC peer grouping, the System Office had concerns about the ability of college administrators (i.e., the chief executive officers, presidents, et al.) to understand the peer grouping idea and the cluster analysis method. The idea and statistics behind it could conceivably have alienated executives because of its "black box" quality. As a remedy for this potential problem, the System Office worked with institutional researchers at the colleges to emphasize and facilitate their role in explaining these technical points to executives, hopefully allaying their suspicion, discomfort and opposition regarding the peer grouping approach. Because a large proportion of the institutional researchers at the colleges had some exposure beforehand (i.e., graduate school coursework) with cluster analysis, their technical assistance (counseling) at the local level apparently diminished the potential problems that the esoteric nature of this approach could have generated. In fact, institutional researchers often played the role of presenters or co-presenters of the ARCC data before local trustees, and they often had to explain the cluster analysis to these elected officials.

It is noteworthy that the ARCC project started in 2004 with a proposal for accountability that a national panel of experts helped to produce (Chancellor's Office, 2007). Although the panel of experts had no involvement in the development of the peer grouping, the set of performance indicators in the ARCC clearly benefited from their input and support at the outset. Their comments and endorsement of the basic plan lent critical credibility to the accountability plan that eventually included a peer grouping component. In addition, the System Office worked to put everyone's focus on all of the report's data rather than on the unique comparisons created with the peer grouping. As one would expect, the news media tended to focus upon the peer group results because of its comparative aspects. Because of a unique set of circumstances, college officials actually publicly promoted peer group results and the ARCC rather than trying to let the ARCC occur with minimal public awareness. These elements of expert input from around the nation and the unique press/media environment that occurred in 2007 may make the California experience somewhat special.

Conclusion

California's use of peer grouping may serve as a useful "test case" in community college accountability across the nation. When state legislatures seek to closely examine the performance of their community college systems, they may refer to California's experience with peer grouping as a possible model for their own version of college accountability. Nevertheless, as time unfolds, the long-term benefits (and costs) of California's peer grouping, along with its own unique political and social climate, will determine how, and if, peer grouping will continue as a tool in California's program for accountability, ARCC. If peer grouping in California were to fall into disfavor to the extent that an impasse over its use occurs, then some form of ranking could possibly replace peer grouping. Naturally, the likelihood that any ranking system could supplant the peer grouping approach would depend upon how legislators and state officials view the feasibility and public appeal of a ranking system (or any other alternative method for performance evaluation for that matter). An abandonment of peer grouping may not occur at all, of course, if the stakeholders in the system (local voters, state oversight bodies, and college officials) can see a net benefit from the peer grouping and both validity and fairness in this approach.

It seems unlikely that college officials will advocate an end to peer grouping. Peer grouping is essentially a substitute for hierarchical ranking of colleges. The latter option has little support among college officials (Phillipe and Boggs, 2003; McClenney, 2007), while classification systems (like peer grouping) do have support. Technically speaking, the peer grouping system in California cannot transform into a ranking system either. Because the cluster analysis produces "clusters" of colleges that constitute a so-called categorical (or nominal) variable, no one can sort the clusters to create a state-wide ranking of the colleges. Any one of the six clusters in an ARCC peer grouping has no logical "position" relative to the other five clusters; the clusters (and thus the colleges) cannot be sorted into a meaningful sequence outside of their peer group. Therefore, the use of cluster analysis for peer grouping does not create a "path" to a hierarchical ranking of the colleges, a quality that would tend to maintain the support of college officials.

In terms of parties that want to consider the adoption of a peer grouping system, we note the following point from Bailey (2003): "…Although each of the classification systems presented in this volume can be used to generate interesting and important insights, classification systems need to be much more systematically defined, and the link between those goals and the measures proposed need to be clearly articulated…. But since different goals will in all likelihood be best served by different schemes, it makes sense either to propose a variety of systems or to provide easily available data that can be used to generate many systems. If we are looking for a system that can be used to benchmark practices, it will be different from one used to distribute money or to help select a sample of community colleges for a research project…." The California peer grouping effort implemented the concept of peer groupings for specific purposes, but the mechanism that it developed for a general accountability plan (i.e., reporting comparisons of performance indicators) may not work for a state that has a different purpose for its peer grouping (i.e., funding or research).

A final thought relates to the capacity of community colleges and their state (central) offices. The use of cluster analysis linked to multiple regression for an official peer grouping effort mandated by the legislature can succeed despite the complexity of this concept. That is, community college systems can succeed at implementing a relatively sophisticated performance measurement system even though senior-level officials may have little technical expertise in the selected methodology. Moreover, a critical element of success for a sophisticated performance measurement system is the participation of technically proficient staff in the community college system (at the local college and central office levels). If California's community colleges had lacked a cadre of qualified researchers, the peer grouping system would probably have faltered in the discussion stage – far short of implementation.

References

Aldenderfer, M.S., & Blashfield, R.K. (1984). *Cluster analysis.* Thousand Oaks, California: Sage.

Bailey, T.R. (2003). A researcher's perspective. In A.C. McCormick & R.D. Cox (Eds.) New directions for community colleges. (pp. 93-100). San Francisco: Jossey-Bass.

California Department of Education. (2007, March). Overview of California's 2006 similar schools ranks based on the API. Retrieved from http://www.cde.ca.gov/ta/ac/ap/documents/simschl06b.pdf

Carnegie Foundation for the Advancement of Teaching. (2007, October). The Carnegie classification of institutions of higher education. Retrieved from http://www.carnegiefoundation.org/classifications/

Chancellor's Office, California Community Colleges. (2007, March). Focus on results: accountability reporting for the community colleges. Retrieved from http://www.cccco.edu/divisions/tris/rp/ab_1417/ARCC_Report_2007.pdf.

Everitt, B.S., Landau, S., & Leese, M. (2001). Cluster analysis. London: Arnold.

Gill, A.M. & Leigh, D.E. (2004). Evaluating academic programs in California's community colleges. San Francisco: Public Policy Institute of California.

Goan, S.K., & Cunningham, A.F. (2007). Differential Characteristics of 2-Year Postsecondary Institutions (NCES 2007-164). U.S. Department of Education. Washington, DC: National Center for Education Statistics.

Hair, J.F. Jr., & Black, W.C. (2000) Cluster analysis. Chapter 5 in L.G.Grimm & P. R. Yarnold (Eds.). *Reading and understanding more multivariate statistics.* (pp.147-205).Washington, D.C.: American Psychological Association.

Han, J., and Kamber, M. (2001). Data mining:concepts and techniques. San Francisco: Morgan Kaufmann.

Hand, D., Mannila, H., and Smyth, P. (2001). Principles of data mining. Cambridge, Massachussets: MIT.

Hurley, R.G. (2002). Identification and assessment of community college peer institution selection systems. *Community College Review.* 29, 1-27.

Legislative Analyst's Office. (2007, November). Update on partnership for excellence. Retrieved from http://www.lao.ca.gov/analysis_2002/education/ed_30_6870_anl02.htm#_Toc1448328

Lorr, M. (1987). Cluster analysis for social scientists. San Francisco: Jossey-Bass.

McClenney, K. (2007, November). Rankled by rankings: point. Retrieved from http://www.ccweek.com/news/templates/template.aspx?articleid=159&zoneid=7

McCormick, A.C., & Zhao, C. (2005). Rethinking and reframing the Carnegie Classification. *Change.* September/October, 51-57.

McCormick, A.C., and Cox, R. D. (2003). Classifying two-year colleges: purposes, possibilities, and pitfalls. In A.C. McCormick & R.D. Cox (Eds.) New directions for community colleges. (pp.7-16). San Francisco: Jossey-Bass.

Mosteller, F., and Tukey, J.W. (1977). Data analysis and regression. Reading, MA: Addison-Wesley.

National Survey of Student Engagement (2007, December). NSSE special analysis product information. Retrieved from http://nsse.iub.edu/special_analysis/index.cfm

Phillipe, K. A. and Boggs, G.R. (2003). The perspective of the American Association of Community Colleges. In A.C. McCormick & R.D. Cox (Eds.) New directions for community colleges. (pp. 79-86). San Francisco: Jossey-Bass.

Phipps, R.A., Shedd, J.M., and Merisotis, J.P. (2001). Classification system for 2-year postsecondary institutions, a. (NCES 2001-167). U.S. Department of Education. Washington, DC: National Center for Education Statistics.

U.S. Department of Education, National Center for Education Statistics. (2007, December). IPEDS peer tool and peer analysis system. Retrieved from http://nces.ed.gov/ipedspas/

Willard Hom *is the director of the Research and Planning Unit at the System Office, California Community Colleges. Before joining the System Office in 1999, he conducted social research for the California Department of Health Services and the California Employment Development Department. He received a bachelor of arts in political science from the University of California, Davis, and a MBA from California State University, Sacramento.*

His recent work has focused on accountability models; his past work has dealt with survey methods, market research and organizational analysis. Willard is also president of the National Community College Council for Research and Planning. He can be reached at 916/327-5887.

A Methodology for Generating Placement Rules that Utilizes Logistic Regression

Keith Wurtz
Chaffey College

The purpose of this article is to provide the necessary tools for institutional researchers to conduct a logistic regression analysis and interpret the results. Aspects of the logistic regression procedure that are necessary to evaluate models are presented and discussed with an emphasis on cutoff values and choosing the appropriate number of candidate predictor variables. In order to demonstrate the process of conducting a logistic regression analysis, models are generated using educational background measures (e.g., last grade in English, high school grade point average, etc.) to predict the dichotomous outcome of success (i.e., grade of A, B, C, or CR) in an English course. At the same time, the information presented here can be applied to other logistic regression studies. Topics covered include setting up the database, dummy coding, data reduction, multicollinearity, missing cases, setting the cutoff value, interpretation of the results, selecting a model, and the interpretation of odds ratios when they are negative.

Introduction

Logistic regression is being used more frequently by institutional researchers conducting educational research across the country (Peng, Lee, & Ingersoll, 2002; DesJardins, 2001). For example, the California Community College Chancellor's Office used logistic regression to identify predictor variables for indicators in the Accountability Reporting for Community Colleges (ARCC). In addition, logistic regression has been used to predict retention of Hispanic/Latino students (Wilson & Hughes, 2006), and to predict college attrition (Zvoch, 2006). Equally important, according to Morest and Jenkins (2007), community colleges are beginning to demand higher level statistical analysis to help with the decision-making process and to identify methods that can help increase student outcomes.

Logistic regression has many advantages over other similar procedures like multiple regression and discriminant analysis (Tabachnick & Fidell, 2007). The advantages of logistic regression are that the candidate predictor variables do not have to be normally distributed, linearly related, or have equal variances (Mertler & Vannatta, 2005). In addition, the candidate predictor variables can be continuous, discrete, and/or dichotomous. Even with all of these advantages, there are some limitations to logistic regression. For instance, the ratio of the number of candidate predictor variables to the number of cases can be problematic if there are too few cases (Mertler & Vannatta, 2005). This limitation and others are discussed in the sections that follow.

Logistic regression has the potential to be a powerful tool in predicting dichotomous outcomes (Peng et al., 2002). A dichotomous outcome is one that can be coded into one of two mutually exclusive categories, e.g., students who earn grades on record (or grades) as compared to those who do not or students who persist from fall to fall versus those who do not. As an illustration, a research study with a dichotomous outcome might involve identifying educational background characteristics to inform decision makers during enrollment management planning.

Conducting logistic regression requires that researchers are at a minimum familiar with both evaluating the validity of a model and the steps to conducting a logistic regression analysis. The methodology used to predict a dichotomous outcome is extremely important because of the impact that the models have on students. For example, if the model does not do well at predicting success, students may take courses that they don't need resulting in increased education costs as well as additional time to reach their goals.

Many community college researchers are responsible for validating third-party assessments like College Board's ACCUPLACER. This paper discusses the process of using logistic regression to predict success in an English course based on educational background measures and assessment scores. This example was chosen because it allows the most thorough review of the options provided by the logistic regression technique. Accordingly, the purpose of this paper is to provide the tools necessary to conduct a logistic regression analysis and to correctly interpret the results.

Research Design

Perhaps the most important aspect of conducting any study is setting up the database and/or the research design. The methodology used to setup the database is extremely important, because it determines the results of the analysis and the meaning of the results. The following examines the processes of choosing the number of candidate predictor variables, selecting cases, setting the cutoff value, dummy coding, controlling for multicollinearity, and working with missing data.

Choosing the Number of Candidate Variables

There are two techniques for reducing the number of candidate variables to ensure that there are sufficient variables in relation to the number of cases. One involves the use of the chi-square statistic and the other uses a formula to control for overfitting the model in relation to the number of cases. The indication that there are too many candidate predictor variables is related to the number of cases (Harrell, 2001; Peduzzi, Concato, Kemper, Holford, & Feinstein, 1996). It is important to reduce the number of candidate predictor variables, because a high number of predictor variables can lead to a model that over fits the data (Harrell). Overfitting is another way of saying that the model is too complex in relation to the number of candidate predictors and the number of cases.

Two techniques were used in this demonstration to reduce the number of candidate predictor variables to avoid overfitting. First, the candidate predictor variables can be reduced by examining whether or not the chi-square statistic is significant at the .05 level when cross tabulating the candidate predictors with success (see Table 1). Again, the data reduction process is important to avoid overfitting of the model. In addition, the reading and sentence scores were examined for statistically significant differences using the t statistic. The independent samples t-test was used because the variables for reading and sentence skills are continuous. This process reduced the number of candidate predictor variables from 84 to 34.

To further control for overfitting, a formula that Harnell (2001) developed from Peduzzi et al.'s (1996) simulation study was used to identify the number of allowable candidate predictor variables: $p < m/10$, e.g., where p is the number of candidate predictors and m is the number of cases required in each group of the dependent variables. In Table 1, the non-success group had the lowest number of cases (i.e., 981) in the dependent variable. Using the formula $p < 981/10$, $p < 98.1$, it was apparent that the number of candidate predictor variables allowed in the model was 98. The current number of 34 candidate predictors was lower than 98 and therefore, is an acceptable number to include in the initial model.

Selecting Cases

1. Students were selected who earned grades on record (i.e., A, B, C, D, F, CR, NC, I, or W) in an English course between Fall 1999 and Spring 2006.

Table 1. Descriptive Statistics p-Values for the Significant & Non-Significant Dummy Coded Candidate Predictor Variables for Success in ENGL-450 with a Score from 70.5-94.4 on the Sentence Meaning Assessment Test

Dummy Coded Candidate Predictor Variables	Not Successful n = 981 (39.0%)	Successful n = 1,536 (61.0%)	p-Value(X^2)
Time out of School			
Still in school	175 (17.8%)	402 (26.2%)	p < .001***
Out of school for less than a year	693 (70.6%)	1,089 (70.9%)	p = .890
Out of school for 2 years or less	825 (84.1%)	1,224 (79.7%)	p = .006*
Out of school for 4 years or less	886 (90.3%)	1,316 (85.7%)	p = .001**
Out of school for 9 years or less	934 (95.2%)	1,411 (91.9%)	p = .001**
Years of High School English			
Less than 1 year	7 (0.7%)	20 (1.3%)	p = .162
1 year or less	24 (2.4%)	52 (3.4%)	p = .179
2 years or less	82 (8.4%)	148 (9.6%)	p = .278
3 years of less	177 (18.0%)	292 (19.0%)	p = .543
Last English Grade			
"F"	21 (2.1%)	13 (0.8%)	p = .006**
"D" or lower	110 (11.2%)	84 (5.5%)	p < .001***
"C" or lower	499 (50.9%)	527 (34.3%)	p < .001***
"B" or lower	873 (89.0%)	1,231 (80.1%)	p < .001***
Planned Weekly Work Hours			
Does not plan to work	117 (11.9%)	282 (18.4%)	p < .001***
10 hours or less	192 (19.6%)	405 (26.4%)	p < .001***
20 hours or less	415 (42.3%)	803 (52.3%)	p < .001***
30 hours or less	744 (75.8%)	1,233 (80.3%)	p = .008**
40 hours or less	950 (96.8%)	1,498 (97.5%)	p = .304
Self-Reported High School GPA			
1.0 or higher	971 (99.0%)	1,531 (99.7%)	p = .027*
1.5 or higher	942 (96.0%)	1,511 (98.4%)	p < .001***
2.0 or higher	803 (81.9%)	1,398 (91.0%)	p < .001***
2.5 or higher	501 (51.1%)	1,061 (69.1%)	p < .001***
3.0 or higher	192 (19.6%)	600 (39.1%)	p < .001***
3.5 or higher	34 (3.5%)	134 (8.7%)	p < .001***

*p < .05, **p < .01, ***p < .001.

2. The file was sorted by student ID and term.
3. The file was unduplicated by grade on record with hierarchical preference assigned to the grade on record that the student earned in his/her first English course. Of the 24,832 grades earned from Fall 1999 to Spring 2006, there was 18,181 or 73% that represented the first English course where a student earned a grade.
4. The assessment data were merged with the first English grade data. It is important to include in the merge the test date and any student demographic and educational background measures
5. The next step in setting up the database involved the creation of a new field from the variable that identifies the start date of the term.

There are two reasons for doing step 5. First, in order to determine the impact of the course placement on student success, students who assessed after the start date of the term were excluded from the analysis. Second, a variable needs to be computed that includes students who were tested within 12 months of the start date of the term. In a quasi-experimental environment, it is important to attempt to have some control over the relationship between the assessment and performance in the course. If students were tested more than a year prior to taking their first English course, this could influence the results of their performance in the course.

Students were selected for this analysis if they had a placement recommendation for any English course for the Fall 2003, 2004, and 2005 or Spring 2004, 2005, and 2006 and earned a grade in that English course. Summer term grades were not used because these have a tendency to be inflated at this community college. For instance, the success rate in English courses in the summer terms ($M = 78.62$, $SD = 41.012$) was statistically significantly higher, $t(1901.26) = -15.153$, $p < .001$, $\eta = .11$, than the success rate in the English courses in the fall and spring terms ($M = 60.62$, $SD = 48.862$). The first English course in which the student earned a grade was used so that other English coursework would not influence results. Furthermore, three years of primary terms were used because there had not been any changes to the placement rules for the ACCUPLACER Sentence Skills Assessment Test during that time. This ensures generating models with the same placement rules.

Setting the Cutoff Value

The feature of setting the cutoff value in logistic regression can be an extremely valuable tool when attempting to predict success or other dichotomous performance outcome measures. The cutoff value is the probability of obtaining a "1" (i.e., successful ENGL-450 course completion). By default in SPSS, if the predicted probability of being successful in ENGL-450 is higher than .50, then the case is classified in the target group (Wright, 1995). If the probability is less than .50, then the case is classified in the non-successful group. The cut-off value directly impacts the results generated for the classification tables. Classification tables compare the predicted ENGL-450 success values with the actual observed values and show the overall prediction accuracy of the model (Mertler & Vannatta, 2005). Usually, the cutoff value is set at the default of .50. However, in this case, it is advisable to set the cutoff value to match the current probability of ENGL-450 success, because the model used needs to exceed this success rate or it's not worthwhile. In this example, the current ENGL-450 success rate is 61%, hence the cutoff value was set at .61.

Dummy Coding

Next, all of the educational background measures need to be dummy coded because they are all ordinal variables. Dummy coding includes the process of transforming responses to a question as either "1," indicating that the respondent has the characteristic, or "0," indicating that the respondent did not have the characteristic. As an illustration, the first educational background question shown in Table 1 asked students how long they had been out of school. Students were able to choose from the following responses: still in school, less than 1 year, 1-2 years, 3-4 years, 5-9 years, or 10 or more years. Each of these responses was dummy coded. For instance, "still in school" was coded as "1" and all of the other responses were coded as "0." Next, less than 1 year was coded as "1" and all of the other responses were coded as "0." Each response was dummy coded in this way. Some researchers use the feature in logistic regression that automatically dummy codes a categorical predictor variable by selecting a referent category. Rather than selecting one category to compare every other category, it makes more sense to compare each category to all other responses as is outlined above. As a result, there are now six variables instead of one with each category having a value of "1" to represent students with that characteristic.

Controlling and Testing for Multicollinearity

Logistic regression analyses assume that the candidate predictor variables are not correlated (Tabachnick & Fidell, 2007; George & Mallery, 2006; Pallant, 2005; SPSS Training, 2001). In order to determine whether or not multicollinearity exists between variables, use the "enter" method in the multiple regression analysis SPSS 15.0.1 to generate the collinearity diagnostics. These collinearity diagnostics produce standardized beta coefficients and tolerance statistics. If multicollinearity exists between any of these variables, the standardized beta coefficients will be higher than 1 (Pallant, 2005; SPSS Training, 2001) and/or the tolerance levels will be .01 or lower (Tabachnick & Fidell, 2007). One can be reasonably sure that multicollinearity does not exist when the standardized beta coefficient is lower than 1 and the tolerance levels are higher than .01.

The first step in testing for multicollinearity is to select a cut-score range that corresponds to the content validity analysis in one specific course. In California, the cut-score range is identified by the content validation process engaged in by the faculty. The faculty identify the range that best corresponds to the skills necessary to be successful in a corresponding course. For instance, at Chaffey College, the English course one level below transfer is ENGL-450. The cut-score range set by faculty for ENGL-450 is 70.5-94.4. Accordingly, for this example, there were 2,517 students who enrolled in this course within a 12-month period after taking the assessment test and earned a grade in ENGL-450 during the primary terms from Fall 2003 to Spring 2006.

Next, after the cases have been selected, the multiple regression analysis in SPSS was used to produce the collinearity diagnostics (i.e., standardized beta coefficients and tolerance statistics). The dichotomous dependent variable (i.e., success in course) was moved into the dependent window and all of the candidate predictor variables were moved into the independent window. The method is "enter" because the purpose of running the multiple regression analysis is to identify multicollinearity. Lastly, under "statistics," the collinearity diagnostics choice needs to be checked. The results of the multiple regression analysis are not important. The standardized beta coefficients and the tolerance statistics in the coefficients output are the only parts of the output that needs to be examined.

The first step in examining the collinearity diagnostics generated from the output involves examining the sentence skills, math assessment, and reading scores. The variable that needs to remain in the analysis is the sentence skills score because of its importance in examining the impact of this score on the success of students (see Figure 1). On the other hand, the sentence skills score is already included in the effect on success in ENGL-450 because of the content validation conducted by the faculty to generate the cut-score range. If the sentence skills score has a standardized beta higher than 1, it is usually because of other assessment scores. The math score beta values are higher than 1, so the next step is to exclude all but the sentence skills and reading score variables. After doing this and re-running the collinearity diagnostics, none of the beta coefficients or tolerance statistics indicated the existence of multicollinearity.

Missing Cases

In community college research, missing cases can be a major problem. Missing cases among the candidate predictor variables can dramatically reduce the probability that the model generated is accurate. For this reason, the replacement of missing cases is recommended over generating a model when valid cases are lost. As long as the cases that are missing are randomly associated with the dependent variable, then it is not only acceptable but preferable to replace the missing cases (Tabachnick & Fidell, 2007; Harrell, 2001). Consequently, all candidate predictor variables were first examined for missing data. If variables had missing data for more than 5% of the cases, they were tested for randomness (Mertler & Vannatta, 2005). Finally, if the data were randomly missing, then the missing data were randomly replaced proportionately with 0s and 1s. Equally important, if the missing data were not random, the variable was excluded from the analysis. For a more in-depth discussion of replacing missing values, see Harrell.

Coefficients[a]

Model		Unstandardized Coefficients B	Std. Error	Standardized Coefficients Beta	t	Sig.	Collinearity Statistics Tolerance	VIF
1	(Constant)	-4.561	27.218		-.168	.882		
	longessy Most writing experience is writing long essays	1.965	2.836	1.994	.693	.560	.003	326.625
	arith	-.049	.124	-1.108	-.396	.731	.003	309.229
	elemalg	.065	.248	.844	.262	.818	.002	409.258
	clm	.044	.083	1.678	.535	.646	.003	388.113
	read	-.007	.065	-.263	-.115	.919	.005	205.506
	ss	.111	.204	1.416	.546	.640	.004	264.673

a. Dependent Variable: successKW Success

Figure 1. Partial coefficients table generated by the linear regression procedure in SPSS 15.0.1 showing the standardized beta coefficients and the tolerance statistic.

When examining the 34 candidate predictor variables nearly all had 1% or less of missing data. The only candidate predictor variable with more than 1% of missing data was the variable of those who spent 2 hours or less a week reading (591 cases or 23% were missing). Consequently, the success rate of those who had missing values was compared to the success rate of all valid values for those who answered the question of how many hours a week they spent reading. It is important to note that the reason there are missing values for this question is that this question was added to the background measures in October of 2003, approximately two years after the use of ACCUPLACER was first instituted. The t-statistic was used to determine if the success rate was statistically significantly different for those with missing data and those with non-missing data for the variable, the number of hours students spent reading (Tabachnick & Fidell, 2007). The respondents, who had valid data on the number of weekly hours spent reading ($M = 61.11$, $SD = 48.762$), did not have a statistically significantly higher success rate than the respondents who had missing data ($M = 60.74$, $SD = 48.873$), $t (2,515) = -.160$, $p = .873$, $\eta = .00$. Hence, the missing data were randomly replaced with the same proportion of 0s and 1s found in the valid data for those who spent two hours or less on reading each week (i.e., 0), and those who spent three or more hours a week reading (i.e., 1). The transformation can be checked by running a simple frequency distribution of the original and transformed variable to examine whether the proportion of cases is the same for both the original and transformed variable.

Results of Logistic Regression

In this particular logistic regression example, the following features from the binary logistic regression are useful in interpreting the results: the method (Forward: Wald), classification plots, Hosmer-Lemeshow goodness-of-fit, CI for exp (B), the classification cutoff, probabilities, and the group membership options. The Wald statistic was chosen because it is more efficient than other methods (Harrell, 2001).

Selecting a Model

In this particular analysis there were 10 models generated that predicted success in ENGL-450. It is important not to simply select the 10th model and assume that this was the best predictor of successfully completing ENGL-450. Since, in this example, the most important aspect is being able to predict success in ENGL-450, it is prudent to examine the classification table to identify the model that best predicts success (see Figure 2). The model that best predicts success was Model 6. When the predicted probability of classifying a student into the target group of successfully completing ENGL-450 was .61 or higher, the model correctly classified 68.5% of the students who were successful.

Next, the Hosmer-Lemeshow goodness-of-fit statistic needed to be checked from Model 6 to ensure that it was not significant. A nonsignificant result indicates that the model is a reliable one (Tabachnick & Fidell, 2007). In this case Model 6 was not significant, $\chi^2 (8) = 12.188$, $p = .143$, which indicates that the model was reliable.

Classification Table

	Observed		0 Not Successful	1 Successful	Percentage Correct
Step 1	Success	0 Not Successful	788	192	80.4
		1 Successful	936	600	39.1
	Overall Percentage				55.2
Step 2	Success	0 Not Successful	712	268	72.7
		1 Successful	769	767	49.9
	Overall Percentage				58.8
Step 3	Success	0 Not Successful	712	268	72.7
		1 Successful	769	767	49.9
	Overall Percentage				58.8
Step 4	Success	0 Not Successful	730	250	74.5
		1 Successful	798	738	48.0
	Overall Percentage				58.3
Step 5	Success	0 Not Successful	677	303	69.1
		1 Successful	681	855	55.7
	Overall Percentage				60.9
Step 6	Success	0 Not Successful	552	428	56.3
		1 Successful	484	1052	68.5
	Overall Percentage				63.8
Step 7	Success	0 Not Successful	650	330	66.3
		1 Successful	628	908	59.1
	Overall Percentage				61.9
Step 8	Success	0 Not Successful	638	342	65.1
		1 Successful	606	930	60.5
	Overall Percentage				62.3
Step 9	Success	0 Not Successful	632	348	64.5
		1 Successful	593	943	61.4
	Overall Percentage				62.6
Step 10	Success	0 Not Successful	631	349	64.4
		1 Successful	594	942	61.3
	Overall Percentage				62.5

a. The cut value is .610

Figure 2. Classification table showing the predicted ENGL-450 values as compared to the observed values and the percent of cases correctly classified when the probability of classifying a student in the target group is .61.

Subsequently, it is best to check the impact of the full model in relation to the constant-only model. A test of Model 6 with six predictors (i.e., out of school for less than a year or more, last English grade was a B or A, works 21 or more hours a week, high school GPA is 2.0 or higher, high school GPA is 3.0 or higher, and 5 years or less since last math class) against the constant-only model was statistically significant, χ^2 (6, N = 2,516) = 213.86, $p < .001$, indicating that the predictors, as a set, reliably distinguished between students who successfully completed ENGL-450 and those who did not (see Table 2).

Interpreting the Individual Predictors. The value of the coefficient β determines the direction of the relationship between the predictor variable and the dependent variable (Peng et al., 2002). For example, the β sign for being out of school for less than a year or more was negative, indicating that being in school was more likely to lead to a successful grade in ENGL-450 (see Table 2). In contrast, the β sign for the last English grade of a B or an A was positive, indicating that earning a B or an A in the student's previous English course was more likely to lead to a successful grade in ENGL-450.

The odds ratios indicate the change in odds of being successful in ENGL-450 when the value of the predictor variable increases by one unit (Tabachnick & Fidell, 2007). As an illustration, the odds of successfully completing ENGL-450 were over 2 times higher for students who had a self-reported GPA of 3.0 or higher in high school (see Table 2). Another method of interpreting the odds ratios involves determining the percent in which the odds of an outcome increase (Tabachnick & Fidell; Peng et al). Hence, if the odds of successfully completing ENGL-450 were 2.2, then the odds of successfully completing ENGL-450 increase by 120% for students who have a self-reported high school GPA of 3.0 or higher.

Interpreting Negative Odds Ratios. Referring to Table 2, three of the predictor variables had negative regression coefficients (i.e. β). Notice that the odds ratios with negative regression coefficients are less than 1. Using the inverse odds ratio (i.e., 1/logg odds) demonstrated by DesJardins (2001), one can calculate the impact of the predictor variable on the outcome. For example, the odds ratio for being out of school for less than a year or more was .662. The inverse odds ratio was 1/.662, which equals 1.51. Consequently, students who were still in school were 1 ½ times more likely to successfully complete ENGL-450.

Conclusion

Limitation. The best method to evaluate logistic regression models is not only to include the Wald test and Hosmer & Lemeshow's goodness-of-fit test, but to also include the likelihood ratio test and the score test (Tabachnick & Fidell, 2007; Peng et al., 2002). Currently, the likelihood ratio test and the score test are not available in the standard package of SPSS; although SPSS does offer the likelihood ratio test in SPSS NOMREG (Tabachnick & Fidell, 2007). For a detailed description on how to include the additional tests in an evaluation of a model, see Tabachnick & Fidell and/or Peng et al.

Benefits of Using Logistic Regression. The ability to use candidate predictor variables that do not require normality, linearity, and equal variances is valuable to institutional researchers. A goal for institutional researchers is to provide constituents with information to help in the

Table 2. Logistic Regression Analysis of Success in English that is One Level below Transfer Level as a Function of Educational Background Measures

Predictor	β	Wald X^2	p	Odd Ratio	95% CI for Odds Ratio	
Out of school for at least one year	-.413	14.901	.000***	.662	.537	.816
Last English grade was "B" or "A"	.335	12.662	.000***	1.398	1.162	1.681
Works 21 or more hours a week	-.397	21.221	.000***	.672	.567	.796
High school GPA is 2.0 or higher	.507	14.178	.000***	1.661	1.275	2.163
High school GPA is 3.0 or higher	.778	55.143	.000***	2.177	1.773	2.674
5 years or less since last math class	-.890	38.519	.000***	.411	.310	.544
Constant	.915	21.857				

Test	X^2	df	p
Overall Model Evaluation			
Wald test	213.862	6	.000***
Goodness-of-fit-test			
Hosmer & Lemeshow	12.188	8	.143

*p < .05, **p < .01, ***p < .001

Note. All variables were coded on a dichotomous scale. For instance, works 21 or more hours a week was coded as "1" and works less than 21 hours a week was coded as "0".

decision-making process. Logistic regression provides this ability in a very dramatic way. Even in this quasi-experimental world, accurate prediction models can be generated that will help identify ways to improve student success, persistence, and enrollment.

References

Brown, E. R., Horton, N. J., & Qian, L. (2004). Use of R as a toolbox for mathematical statistics exploration. *The American Statistician, 58,* 343+. Retrieved January 30, 2007, from the Questia database.

DesJardins, S. L. (2001). A comment on interpreting odds ratios when logistic regression coefficients are negative. *The Association for Institutional Research, 81,* 1-10. Retrieved October, 15, 2006, from http://airweb3.org/airpubs/81.pdf

George, D., & Mallery, P. (2006). *SPSS for windows step by step: A simple guide and reference (6th ed.).* Boston: Allyn and Bacon.

Harrell, F. E. (2001). *Regression modeling strategies: With applications to linear models, logistic regression, and survival analysis.* New York: Springer Science+Business Media, Inc.

Mertler, C. A., & Vannatta, R. A. (2005). *Advanced multivariate statistical methods (3rd ed.): Practical application and interpretation.* Glendale: Pyrczak Publishing.

Morest, V. S., & Jenkins, D. (2007). Institutional research and the culture of evidence at community colleges. *Community College Research Center.* Retrieved August 4, 2007 from http://ccrc.tc.columbia.edu/Publication.asp?UID=515

Pallant, J. (2005). *SPSS survival guide: A step by step guide to data analysis using SPSS version 12 (2nd ed.).* London: McGraw-Hill Education.

Peduzzi, P., Concato, J., Kemper, E., Holford, T. R., & Feinstein, A. R. (1996). A simulation study of the number of events per variable in logistic regression analysis. *Journal of Clinical Epidemiology, 49,* 1373-1379.

Peng, C. Y. J., Lee, K. L., & Ingersoll, G. M. (2002). An introduction to logistic regression analysis and reporting. *The Journal of Educational Research, 96,* 3-14. Retrieved August 1, 2006 from the Academic Search Premier database.

SPSS Training. (2001). *Advanced techniques: Regression.* SPSS Inc.: Chicago.

Tabachnick, B. G., & Fidell, L. S. (2007). *Using multivariate statistics (5th ed.).* Boston: Pearson Education.

Wilson, V. L., & Hughes, J. N. (2006). Retention of Hispanic/Latino students in first grade: Child, parent, teacher, school, and peer predictors. *Journal of School Psychology, 44,* 31-49. Retrieved March 4, 2007 from the Academic Search Premier database.

Wright, R. E. (1995). Logistic regression. In L.G. Grimm and P.R. Yarnold (Eds.), *Reading and Understanding Multivariate Statistics* (pp. 217-244). Washington, D.C.: American Psychological Association.

Zvoch, K. (2006). Freshman year dropouts: Interactions between student and school characteristics and student dropout status. *Journal of Education for Students Placed at Risk, 11,* 97-117. Retrieved March 4, 2007 from the Academic Search Premier database.

Keith Wurtz *is a Walden University graduate student and senior research analyst at Chaffey College in Rancho Cucamonga, CA. He can be reached at keith.wurtz@chaffey.edu.*

Current Lit Abstracts

The Influence of Financial Aid on Community College Students

Eddy A. Ruiz

The following citations for research and resource materials focus on the influence of financial aid on community college students.

Introduction

Fiscal resources are vital to many minority and low-income students who attend two-year institutions. Federal, state, and institutional aid impact student retention, degree attainment, college choice, and access. Not all financial aid is created equal or yields the same outcomes. The following resources are pertinent because the majority of studies have focused primarily on four-year institutions. The research presented provides national data sets and case studies that utilized qualitative and quantitative measures to analyze distinct financial aid resources as they related to community college students. The findings have broad implications for administration, advising, and policy makers as their outcomes influence enrollment trends, labor markets, and educational equity.

ERIC documents (references with "ED" numbers) may be read on microfiche at approximately 900 libraries worldwide. In addition, the full text of many documents is available online at http://www.eric.ed.gov. Journal articles may be acquired through regular library channels, from the originating journal publisher, or for a fee from the following article reproduction vendor, Ingenta; email: ushelp@ingenta.com, phone: 617-395-4046, toll-free: 1-800-296-2221, URL: http://www.ingenta.com.

Dowd, A. C., & Coury, T. (2006). Effect of loans on the persistence and attainment of community college students. *Research in Higher Education 47*(1), 33-62.

This study examines public policies regarding the use of subsidized loans as financial aid for community college students. Using logistic regression, it analyzes the National Center for Education Statistics' Beginning Postsecondary Students (BPS 90/94) data to predict persistence to the second year of college and associate's degree attainment over five years. During the period under study, loans did not contribute to higher persistence and attainment rates. Loans are observed to have a negative effect on persistence and no effect on degree attainment. Estimates of the interaction effects of borrowing and income status are insignificant but demonstrate the need for further testing. The findings are attributed to a combination of the high uncertainty of degree completion among community college students and the negative affective component of indebtedness.

Gladieux, L., & Perna, L. (2005). *Borrowers who drop out: A neglected aspect of the college student loan trend* (National Center Report No. 05-2). The National Center for Public Policy and Higher Education: San Jose, CA.

Borrowers Who Drop Out is an important contribution to the National Center's and the nation's understanding of students who aspire to earn educational certificates and degrees, but do not achieve their goals—and yet are saddled with significant debt to repay. The researchers utilized the most recent and comprehensive data available from the U.S. Department of Education on students who first enrolled in postsecondary education in 1995-96, with a snapshot of the same students in 2001. The findings are revealing, if not disturbing. Half of the students who enrolled in postsecondary education in 1995-96, also borrowed in 1995-96; more than 20% of those students dropped out of their educational programs, yet were burdened with significant debt. They had, in effect, the worst of both worlds—they did not benefit from the higher income associated with education beyond high school, and they accumulated significant educational debt. Many of these students were unemployed in 2001 and defaulted on their loans, thus damaging their credit standing. Most students benefit from loans and are able to repay them when they leave higher education. However, borrowing, combined with other risk factors for not completing higher education (such as working too many hours, lack of adequate preparation, and part-time attendance), puts many students, especially low-income and first-generation students, at a particular disadvantage.

Davids, C. B. (2006). *Financial aid as a predictor of retention at a two-year college.* Unpublished doctoral dissertation, Clemson University, SC.

The primary purpose of this study was to determine the likelihood that the type of financial assistance a student receives is a predictor of retention at a two-year college. The institution utilized in the study is a mid-size, public, two-year college in South Carolina. The effects of five distinct types of financial assistance on retention were investigated. The types of financial assistance included Federal Pell Grant, Legislative Incentive for Future Excellence (LIFE) Scholarship, South Carolina Education Lottery (SCEL) Tuition Assistance, a combination of South Carolina Education Lottery Tuition Assistance and Federal Pell Grant, and a combination of LIFE Scholarship and Federal Pell Grant. Two secondary data sources were also used in the study for the first-time, full-time freshmen in a Fall 2002 cohort. There were 300 participants in this study and a forward stepwise method of binary logistic regression was used to determine the probability of predicting retention with the independent variables. Findings from the study show that the majority, 89.02% of first-time, full-time freshmen attending CCTC in the fall of 2002 received financial assistance. The highest percentage of students received the Federal Pell Grant. Most of the students were female, between the ages of 18 and 25, White/non-Hispanic, and enrolled in an associate's degree program of study. Of the 300 participants, 38% were retained. The analysis of the data indicates that four of the research hypotheses relating to financial assistance was not rejected. The research hypothesis on the demographic variables of age, ethnicity, gender, and program of study was not rejected. The research hypothesis on the financial variable of LIFE Scholarship as a predictor of retention at a two-year college was rejected. The conclusion is that a significant positive relationship exists between financial assistance through the LIFE Scholarship and retention for students at a two-year college.

Bettinger, E. (2004). How financial aid affects persistence. Accessed http://ssrn.com/abstract=492355 on 5/1/2008.

The Pell Grant program is the largest means-tested financial assistance available to postsecondary students across the United States, yet researchers have only limited evidence on the causal effects of these grants. This paper examines the effect of Pell grants on student persistence after the first year. The paper uses unique, student-level data from all public colleges in Ohio. The data include detailed financial statistics which are helpful in identifying small discontinuities in the Pell grant formula and the causal effects of the voucher. The results based on discontinuity approaches suggest that Pell grants reduce college drop-out behavior. The results in this paper support other evidence that find a relationship between need-based aid and college completion (e.g. Dynarski 2002, Turner and Bound 2002).

Rogers, K. R. (2005). *How much does money matter? An examination of the impact of financial aid programs on the sub-baccalaureate degree and certificate attainment of low-income students and adult learners.* Unpublished doctoral dissertation, Pennsylvania State University, University Park.

This dissertation examined the impact of federal, state, and institutional student aid programs on the associate's degree and certificate attainment of low-income students and adult learners. As more than half of all students attend a two-year college at some point during their postsecondary educational experiences, it is important to determine whether student aid affects these students in the same way it influences their counterparts who attend four-year public, private not-for-profit, and for-profit colleges and universities. The study used data from the National Center for Education Statistics' Beginning Postsecondary Students study (BPS: 96/01), of extended current within-year and year-to-year persistence understanding by asking how the college financing package students receive, in concert with their background and academic characteristics, affected the certificate completion and associate degree attainment of low-income students and adult learners. A logistic regression analyses suggested that the receipt of grant aid early in college has a significant positive effect on the sub-baccalaureate credentialing of both low-income students and adult learners. The receipt of a Pell grant during the 1996-97 academic year resulted in low-income students being 81% more likely to attain a sub-baccalaureate credential, while adult learners receiving the same form of aid the same year increased their attainment by 67% over non-recipients. The negative findings with respect to latter years of federal and institution need-based grant assistance for adult learners were most likely attributable to the inadequacy in the amount of aid received, not the receipt of the aid itself. Stafford loan receipt was positively associated with attainment for low-income students during the 1996-97 academic year and for adult learners during the 1999-2000 academic year, respectively. Interestingly, Perkins loan receipt was significant for three academic years, 1997-98, 1998-99, and 2000-01, but only for adult learners. Adult-learner recipients of Perkins loans were significantly more likely to attain a credential if the loan receipt occurred during the 1997-98 academic year, but the effects of the loan were negative for the latter years of receipt.

Redd, K. E. (2004). Lots of money, limited options: College choice and student financial aid. *NASFAA Journal of Student Financial Aid, 34*(3), 29-39.

Financial aid and college preparatory programs are designed in part to allow students from low-income families to have the same choices of institutions as those from middle- and upper-income groups. Unfortunately, despite providing more than $100 billion in financial aid and college preparatory assistance, state and federal policy makers have been unable to achieve the goal of equalizing college choice for students from low- and moderate income families. Throughout the 1990s, these undergraduates became even more likely to enroll at community colleges and lower cost four-year public institutions than their peers from higher-income families. These trends suggest that policy makers have been successful in using financial aid and other policies to improve college access for low-income students, but have been unsuccessful in achieving true equality in college choice. Why have financial aid and academic enrichment programs fallen short of their goal of achieving equal educational opportunity? What options are available to campus officials and state and federal policy makers who want to reverse these trends? This study reviews some of the key reasons increases in grants and other support for low-income students have failed to equalize college choice between low- and higher-income undergraduates, and proposes some solutions for closing the college choice gap.

Denny, D. K. (2007). *Impact of loan indebtedness on economic choices of community college students who earn baccalaureate degrees.* Unpublished doctoral dissertation, University of Illinois, Urbana-Champaign.

This study explored the impact of indebtedness in the Federal Stafford Loan program on economic choices made by baccalaureate graduates of Western Illinois University who began their postsecondary programs at community colleges. A questionnaire was administered using a fifteen-question instrument with three demographic questions and one open-ended question. The purpose of this study was to examine the perceptions of baccalaureate graduates about the impact of indebtedness on their ability to make economic choices. The study found that graduates perceived student loan indebtedness to be a factor in selected economic choices. There was no evidence among respondents that decisions made regarding marriage, having children, or career choice were related to having student loan indebtedness. Approximately four out of ten respondents (41.7%) reported being "extremely satisfied" with their decision to borrow to invest in their education. However graduates with above-average indebtedness were more likely to respond that they were "neutral" to "not at all satisfied" with their decision to borrow (53 of 101 or 52.5%). Slightly more than half of all respondents (51.8%) indicated that they would borrow the same amount to attend college if given the choice again. Only 10.4% responded that they would borrow more if given the chance. More than one third (36.2%) indicated that they would borrow less. Graduates were asked if repaying their student loan had a noticeable impact on their standard of living. Respondents in the aggregate were neutral in their response. When the level of indebtedness of the respondent was considered, a pattern was discerned. A similar result was obtained regarding the question of debt burden. In the aggregate responses were neutral. When the level of indebtedness of the respondent was considered, another pattern was discerned.

Burdman, P. (2005). *The student debt dilemma: Debt aversion as a barrier to college access* **(CSHE.13.05). The Institute for College Access and Success: University of California, Berkeley.**

Though the rise in college student debt often has been blamed on rising tuition, a radical shift in student financial aid—from a system relying primarily on need-based grants to one dominated by loans—has been equally important. Numerous reports have highlighted the burdens faced by students who borrow large sums, but less is known about students who are averse to borrowing. For these students, the increasing prominence of loans could actually narrow their options and decrease their chances of attending and completing college. Given the increasingly important role of student loans in financial aid packages, perceptions about debt influence the ability of loan programs to achieve their goal of equalizing opportunity for students at all income levels. Based on interviews with students, counselors, outreach professionals, and financial aid directors, as well as a review of relevant research, this discussion paper offers an initial gauge of the debt dilemma and recommends four broad strategies: (1) making more grant money available for low-income and first-generation students, (2) making loan programs more attractive and efficient through income-based repayment strategies, (3) better integrating financial aid awareness into high school counseling, and (4) providing more pathways for students who prefer to attend part-time. Loans are likely to remain a mainstay of federal financial aid programs, so as interest rates begin to rise for the first time in years, foreshadowing higher future payments, the problems faced by students who borrow as well as the barriers confronted by those who are averse to borrowing are only liable to increase.

Zumeta, W., & Frankle, D. (2007). *California community colleges: Making them stronger and more affordable* (National Center Report #07-1). National Center for Public Policy and Higher Education: San Jose, CA.

This report highlights the affordability gaps faced by California's community colleges. Despite the lowest tuition in the country and tuition waivers for the lowest-income students, many California students struggle to afford the total cost of education, which includes housing, food, health care, and textbooks. Although California students are generally lower-income than students in other states, fewer of them receive financial aid. As a result, students in California take fewer classes and work longer hours than do students in other states. The report urges strengthening financial aid programs, increasing student utilization of existing financial aid, and using revenues from modest tuition increases to support programs to improve student success. It also cites some practices, including the Board Financial Assistance Program (BFAP), that have been successful in assisting more students in receiving financial aid.

Prince, H. (2006). *Money on the table: State initiatives to improve financial aid participation.* Jobs for the Future: Boston, MA.

Increasing the numbers of students who participate in financial aid programs has become a critical issue for many state systems. Reasons for the low rates of financial aid uptake vary, from lack of awareness among students to the many and complex types of aid available to inadequate capacity at the institutional level for conducting outreach to students and processing financial aid applications. This brief highlights the activities of four states to address this issue, which is central to Achieving the Dream, a national initiative to help more community college students succeed, particularly low-income students and students of color. It draws on experiences in three states that later joined Achieving the Dream—Connecticut, North Carolina, and Texas—as well as California.

Brock, T., & Richburg-Hayes, L. (2006). *Paying for persistence. Early results of a Louisiana scholarship program for low-income parents attending community college.* MDRC: New York, NY.

Community colleges, which tend to be more accessible and affordable than other postsecondary institutions, are a critical resource for low-income people striving to improve their prospects in the labor market and in life. Yet nearly half of students who begin at community colleges leave school before receiving a credential. Research by MDRC (formerly known as Manpower Demonstration Research Corporation) and others suggests that many community college students want to earn a degree but are overwhelmed by the competing demands of work, family, and school. Institutional barriers, such as poorly tailored instruction, insufficient financial aid, or inadequate advising, may also impede their academic progress. In 2003, MDRC launched the Opening Doors demonstration project to study the effects of innovative programs designed to help students stay in school and succeed. Six colleges in four states are taking part in the demonstration. This report presents early findings from Louisiana Opening Doors, an enhanced financial aid program targeting low-income parents at two community colleges in the New Orleans area: Delgado Community College and Louisiana Technical College-West Jefferson. This program was designed to help students with their expenses and provide an incentive to make good academic progress. Students randomly assigned to Opening Doors were offered a $1,000 scholarship for each of two semesters, in addition to the regular financial aid they qualified for, if they enrolled at least half time and earned a C average or higher. They also received enhanced counseling. Students in a control group received only regular financial aid and the counseling available to all students. The early findings in Louisiana are compelling and suggest that a performance-based scholarship can indeed have a positive effect on persistence and academic achievement among a student population that faces multiple barriers to completing college. The students in Opening Doors were more likely to enroll in college full time, passed more courses, earned more course credits, and had higher rates of persistence.

Book Review

Achieving and Sustaining Institutional Excellence for the First Year of College. **Betsy O. Barefoot, John N. Gardner, Marc Cutright, Libby V. Morris, Charles C. Schroeder, Stephen W. Schwartz, Michael J. Siegel, Randy L. Swing.** Jossey-Bass, San Francisco, CA: 2005. 448 pages (ISBN: 0-7879-7151-0)

Bill Scroggins
College of the Sequoias

Accountability. Yes, higher education today is squarely in the crosshairs of those who want results. Government leaders want to justify their dwindling investment in higher education in terms of higher graduation rates. Accreditors are fighting for their very existence and hounding colleges for data on student learning outcomes. High tuition rates are fostering an increasing sense of consumerism among students (and their parent-investors) to be sure they get that sheepskin. As campus leaders, we are under increasing pressure to take those underprepared entering freshmen, clean them up, and get them across the finish line. We can complain and continue to blame high schools — or we can look at research results and published accounts that produce results. Barefoot and Gardner's book is about results: thirteen well researched and documented case studies of a range of colleges that got freshmen through the first year and on to complete their educational goals.

As a college president who was trained as a scientist and institutional researcher, my first inclination when faced with a problem is to look for data. One persistent problem is persistence — the community college's open door is more often a revolving door. Community colleges typically lose about half of their students in the first year. It was a real eye-opener for me to read in Cliff Adelman's seminal research study, *Moving Into Town – and Moving On: The Community College in the Lives of Traditional-age Students*, that "The prize…is getting beyond 20 additive credits by the end of the first calendar year of attendance" (Adelman, 2005, p. 69). So what set of college behaviors can enable students to achieve those 20 units and persist into the second year?

John Gardner is certainly one of the best people to answer that question. He heads the Policy Center on the First Year of College and founded the National Resource Center for The First-Year Experience at the University of South Carolina, originating and teaching USC's University 101 program. His 35 years of experience working to improve the success of first-year students greatly contributed to his work on this book. Here at College of the Sequoias we have used this book, and related works of Professor Gardner and his colleagues, to establish our own successful First Year Experience (FYE) initiative. John has worked closely with our staff in this process, and we can testify that the elements of the case studies in this work are practical and useful in improving student achievement.

The case studies reported in this book originated with proposals from dozens of colleges, which were winnowed down by a team of reviewers using specific criteria. Finalists were subjected to site visits, so the descriptions are rich with first-hand observations. Two of the studies are of community colleges. The two-year schools are LaGuardia Community College in Queens, New York, and the Community College of Denver (CCD). The nine, four-year school case studies are arranged by institutional size. All of the examples have nuggets of insights.

Of CCD, John Roueche, in his 2001 study of the college, lauded their "logical, rational, and commonsense approaches to improving student success" (Roueche, 2001). This certainly emerges in Gardner's profile. Several approaches used by CCD to assist its 13,000 students are notable: assessment is required of all students, academic advising is well utilized through a three-tier delivery mechanism, a case management system actively contacts students about their progress, and all this is done in a flexible and student-oriented manner. The book describes these initiatives in sufficient detail to be useful to the reader who would like to pursue implementation. For example, the second tier of advising consists of referring each student to one or more targeted programs, each of which is described and the results spelled out. The history of how the FYE program at CCD evolved is chronicled, pointing out the importance of visionary leadership from the president and also the importance of institutional research — notably led by a senior cabinet position, the vice president of institutional effectiveness, planning and technology. This office conducts regular research and analysis on aspects of the FYE program at CCD, including a campus climate survey. Interest in such surveys is growing as evidenced by the recently inaugurated Survey of Entering Student Engagement, an off-shoot of the well-established Community College Survey of Student Engagement housed at the University of Texas at Austin (McClenny, 2007). Aspects of the CCD story that may make their journey more difficult for many of us to replicate include their amazing success at securing external funds and the fact that they are located on a downtown Denver site that they share with Metropolitan State College and the University of Colorado at Denver, with many facilities shared among the three institutions.

LaGuardia Community College in the Borough of Queens educates 12,000 credit and 30,000 continuing education students. The LaGuardia story, as told by Gardner and his team, is truly inspiring. Over 90 percent of the college's very diverse students begin at the developmental level. Begun with missionary zeal, LaGuardia has prospered by making well-informed decisions based on solid research. For example, its extensive and varied format learning community system went through some major transformations based on a study of ten years of data representing over 90,000 course sections. As Gardner observes, "The president believes that data are essential in order to survive in the external political climate, and she insists that decisions about the allocation of resources be supported by evidence" (Gardner, 2005, p. 63). The hallmark of the new student experience at LaGuardia is the variety of special programs in which every student can find a place. For example, one of the learning communities, New Student House, block enrolls students in basic reading, basic writing, and the New Student Seminar. Data show that students in learning communities outperform those in stand-alone courses. Another special program is the New Student Seminar. As with the description of initiatives at Community College of Denver, the descriptions here are of sufficient detail—including the pros and cons of the LaGuardia design of the New Student Seminar—to be useful to those who would like to replicate this program at their own colleges. Other special programs include a range of preparatory courses and second chance courses taught during intersessions and in summers, a collegwide mentorship program, and a common reading initiative.

Achieving and Sustaining Institutional Excellence for the First Year of College is a springboard for ideas. Each time I read this book, I gain new insights into projects at my own college and am inspired to recommit myself to the challenging task of creating a supportive learning environment that will get our entering students through and beyond their critical first year of college.

References

Adelman, C. (2005). Moving into town—and moving on: The community college in the lives of traditional-age students. Washington, DC: U.S. Department of Education.

McClenney, K. (2007) Starting right, a first look at engaging entering students. *Community College Survey of Student Engagement.*

Roueche, J.E., Ely, E.E., & Roueche, S.D. (2001). Pursuing excellence: The community college of Denver. *Community College Journal of Research and Practice, 25,* 517-537.

Bill Scroggins *is president/superintendent of College of the Sequoias in Visalia, California.*

2007-2008 Annual Update
Journal of Applied Research in the Community College

Andreea Serban, Ph.D.
Executive Editor

Published Issues

During this past year, the Spring 2007 (vol. 14, no. 2) and Fall 2007 (vol. 15, no.1) issues were published. The Spring 2007 issue included the 2005-06 best papers of NCCCRP and of the Research and Planning Group of California Community Colleges (RP Group).

Issues in Progress

At this time, the Spring 2008 issue is being finalized. This is a special issue focused on assessing institutional effectiveness and student learning outcomes. All articles for the Fall 2008 issue have been identified and are in final editing stages.

Publisher

JARCC remains at New Forums Press, and Dr. Doug Dollar, the publisher, has worked with us to revise the cover and the print quality. In addition, we have worked with Doug on taking *JARCC* online and we are happy to report that the journal is expected to be fully online by the end of the summer. The online presence will significantly increase the exposure and visibility of the journal which will now be indexed in Swets-Blackwell, OCLC, British Library, EBSCO Publishing, EJS, Google, and Harrassowitz. The electronic version of the journal will be available for purchasing either by issue or by individual article.

Managing and Associate Editors

In February 2008, Heather Burns, who served as Managing Editor for the past five years, left this post. Melissa Banks, who served both as associate and copy editor for several years, retired after the completion of the Spring 2008 issue. I would like to extend my heartfelt thanks and appreciation for their exceptional service and dedication to the quality of the journal. Fortunately, Diane Riopka, from South Orange County Community College District in Mission Viejo, California, has accepted to serve both as Managing and Copy Editor for the journal since March 2008. Diane is talented, detail oriented and a great colleague and she is already doing an outstanding job for the journal.

Editorial Advisory Board (EAB)

During 2007-2008, no new members were appointed to the EAB. Board members review manuscripts, advise the editors on the quality of the manuscripts and appropriateness for publication in *JARCC*, and offer critical and helpful feedback to authors. The quality of the journal is in large measure dependent on the efforts of this group. Thank you to all board members for your dedication and service to the journal!

"Mining," Flow and Selection of Manuscripts

The number of manuscripts submitted for review has continued to increase. At this time, we have identified articles for the Spring 2009 issue and have articles under review, some of which will be slated for the Fall 2009 issue. We continue to encourage those presenting at the AIR conference to consider submitting their work to *JARCC*. We work closely with the authors, helping them develop their manuscripts into the publishable quality expected by *JARCC*. Also, we sometimes ask authors to revise their articles significantly to give more emphasis to features or findings that are of most interest to *JARCC* readers.

Article Type

We continue to encourage applied research articles but also look for those with a focus on planning and assessment; those that describe new tools or techniques for use in research, planning and assessment ("Toolbox" articles); special essays; research briefs (e.g., defining variables in a new way, short summary of a research study with implications for how others approach this kind of research at their institution, etc.); and book reviews. With support from Dr. Art Cohen, students in a doctoral program at UCLA will continue to provide *JARCC* with a summary of recent literature pertinent to a particular topic for inclusion in each issue. Rozana Carducci, who has helped *JARCC* for several years, has finished the graduate program and is no longer writing literature abstracts for us. Many thanks to Rozana for the many excellent summaries she provided! Eddy Ruiz, graduate student at UCLA, has taken on the role and has contributed to literature abstracts for the Spring 2008 issue.

In closing I would like to acknowledge the talents and dedication of the group of Associate Editors with whom I have the good fortune to work. Special thanks to Heather Burns and Melissa Banks who have provided excellent service to JARCC for the past several years and to Diane Riopka, who has joined as Managing and Copy Editor, and is already doing a great job for the journal. I would like to acknowledge Dr. Doug Dollar, our publisher, for his continued support for the journal and for taking the journal online this year. Finally, I want to thank all our colleagues in the field who read our journal and provide feedback, ideas and comments.

Dr. Andreea Serban *is Executive Editor of JARCC and Superintendent/President at Santa Barbara City College. She can be reached at serban.andreea.mihaela@gmail.com.*

President's Message

Georgia Gudykunst
Ph.D., President

The National Community College Council for Research and Planning (NCCCRP) has had a busy and challenging year in 2007-08. I would like to take this opportunity to thank all the members of the Executive Board, our Regional Directors and our e-Parameter editor and the editorial board of the Journal of Applied Research in the Community College (JARCC) for all of their hard work and accomplishments this past year. It has been an honor and pleasure to work with this group.

NCCCRP began to look at its constitution and areas where bylaws could be expanded. Several members, including the President-elect Sharon Kristovich, Secretary Karen Laljiani, and I began reviews of bylaws being used by similar groups. We anticipate that NCCCRP will recommend some bylaws to the membership by the end of the 2009 year.

NCCCRP's treasurer, Dr. Pat Vampatella, concluded her two-year term. However, she very graciously continued to serve until an election could be held. Subsequently, the Board decided it was in the best interests of the organization to appoint one of the regional directors to assume the post and serve the remainder of the two year term. We appreciate Pat's dedication and service.

NCCCRP deliberated considerably before raising the membership dues for the 2007-08 year. The Board hesitated due to the tightening of college budgets and competing interests from national, regional and state research organizations for members. In the final analysis, dues were raised in order to cover the rising costs of journal production (editorial assistance needed for production). Board members will include focus in the coming year on supporting this quality journal yet keeping membership fees at current levels.

NCCCRP's journal – JARCC – continues to provide excellent value. The Journal has continued to receive increasing numbers of manuscripts and increasing interest under the leadership of Executive Editor, Dr. Andreea Serban.

NCCCRP membership levels remain relatively steady, but the dues increase may have affected some renewals. Membership Coordinator, Dana Rosenberg, has kept diligent track of members -coming and going from one institution to the next- as well as their region and state affiliations and continues to ask how members would like to assist the organization. (If you want to help in another area than noted originally on your membership form, please feel free to contact any of the officers to let us know how you would like to volunteer.) Secretary Karen Laljiani kept us on track with diligent recording of monthly Executive Board meetings as well as the General Meeting held at the Annual AIR Forum.

Regional Director Mary Day and I obtained AIR membership lists and identified those AIR members who are not members of NCCCRP. We sent out letters of information/welcome to join, and this brought in a few members. NCCCRP will need to continue to market its benefits, including the Journal, collegial interaction and contacts, and e-Parameter to potential members. It was interesting to discover that we have members from most states and regions, but not all. Another market to target would be the academic officers by working with other organizations. I requested a list of names and addresses of Community College Chief Academic Officers and Presidents from AACC; when we receive a list, we can use this in a membership drive.

NCCCRP has learned of new reporting requirements from the IRS. The new treasurer has been busy recently with identifying and preparing the necessary paperwork. We appreciate Qing Mack's dedication in following up on what is needed and advising the Board.

NCCCRP has seen the e-Parameter newsletter on NCCCRP website expand and move forward with new content as well as volunteer reporting from members about their state or regional activities and issues. Some compelling topics have included looking at economic impact analyses and what do these mean for us, and state mandates. We thank Willard Hom for his service. Now I look forward to building e-Parameter upon the foundations set by Willard and predecessors.

NCCCRP continued its work with the American Association of Community Colleges through 29007-08. As President, I served as the NCCCRP representative on the AACC Council of Affiliated Councils and its relatively new Commission on Emerging Trends and Research. NCCCRP now has an agreement that AACC affiliated organizations can post links to research studies conducted by any of the councils on the NCCCRP web site.

In June 2008 a new slate of officers was elected. I appreciate the help of the executive officers with the election process, particularly given the early resignation of the president-elect, one year term of the past-president, and family health issues of the president. The Executive Board officers and the regional directors are identified on the NCCCRP website. http://www.ncccrp.org/page.asp?page=594

As I transition to the office of past-president, I would like to extend my best wishes to President Hom and the new executive board, the regional directors and JARCC editorial staff. It has been a privilege and pleasure to serve as NCCCRP President.

Index of JARCC Back Issues

Vol. & No.	Date
Vol. 1, No. 1	Summer 1993
Vol. 1, No. 2	Spring 1994
Vol. 2, No. 1	Fall 1994
Vol. 2, No. 2	Spring 1995
Vol. 3, No. 1	Fall 1995
Vol. 3, No. 2	Spring 1996
Vol. 4, No. 1	Fall 1996
Vol. 4, No. 2	Spring 1997
Vol. 5, No. 1	Fall 1997
Vol. 5, No. 2	Spring 1998
Vol. 6, No. 1	Fall 1998
Vol. 6, No. 2	Spring 1999
Vol. 7, No. 1	Fall 1999
Vol. 7, No. 2	Spring 2000
Vol. 8, No. 1	Fall 2000
Vol. 8, No. 2	Spring 2001
Vol. 9, No. 1	Fall 2001
Vol. 9, No. 2	Spring 2002
Vol. 10, No. 1	Fall 2002
Vol. 10, No. 2	Spring 2003
Vol. 11, No. 1	Fall 2003
Vol. 11, No. 2	Spring 2004
Vol. 12, No. 1	Fall 2004
Vol. 12, No. 2	Spring 2005
Vol. 13, No. 1	Fall 2005
Vol. 13, No. 2	Spring 2006
Vol. 14, No. 1	Fall 2006
Vol. 14, No. 2	Spring 2007
Vol. 15, No. 1	Fall 2007
Vol. 15, No. 2	Spring 2008

Submissions: Information For Contributors

The *Journal of Applied Research in the Community College* publishes applied research articles as well as those that describe innovative approaches and models for use in planning and assessment in community colleges. *JARCC* is also interested in "toolbox" articles, those that describe in some detail a specific technique (e.g., a data collection instrument or approach, an analytic technique, a way to communicate data to decision makers, etc.) that can improve research, planning and assessment practices in community colleges; special essays where the author(s) take a particular point of view; and book reviews.

Manuscripts should generally be 10-20 pages in length (double-spaced) and should be sent to the Executive Editor in a Word document by e-mail. Each manuscript should be accompanied by an abstract of 150 words or less, along with the address, phone number, e-mail address and FAX number for the lead author. Each table and figure should be saved as a Word document in a separate file with an indication in the article of about where each should be placed. Images created in pdf must be converted to jpg or tif and Excel tables must be converted to Word. Manuscripts submitted to the journal must not be under consideration by other publishers. All manuscripts should conform to the guidelines as outlined in the *APA Style Manual, 5th Edition*.

Articles are screened initially by one of the editors for appropriateness with the purposes of JARCC and overall quality. If the screening is positive, then the article is sent out for blind peer review to two members of the Editorial Advisory Board (see listing). The criteria used in the review process include the following: makes a significant contribution to administration, policy making and/or the practice of institutional research at community colleges; generates reader interest; represents a timely topic; clearly defines and states the problem; makes a clear link to previous literature; uses appropriate design and methodology; logically organizes the presentation; writes clearly, and provides conclusions/implications/recommendations substantiated by the content presented. If, after review, the article is accepted for publication, the Executive Editor will assign an Associate Editor to work with the author(s) on any revisions that are requested.

If you have presented at a local, regional or national conference and are wondering if your work might be appropriate for consideration by *JARCC*, we encourage you to contact the Executive Editor via e-mail. An important purpose of the journal is to encourage more community college institutional researchers, planners and assessment specialists to consider sharing their good work through formal publication.

Send manuscripts to Andreea M. Serban, Executive Editor, at serban.andreea.mihaela@gmail.com

Made in the USA